Robert Williams Buchanan

The Devil's Case

A bank holiday interlude

Robert Williams Buchanan

The Devil's Case
A bank holiday interlude

ISBN/EAN: 9783337123819

Printed in Europe, USA, Canada, Australia, Japan

Cover: Foto ©Suzi / pixelio.de

More available books at **www.hansebooks.com**

THE DEVIL'S CASE

𝔄 𝔅𝔞𝔫𝔨 ℌ𝔬𝔩𝔦𝔡𝔞𝔶 𝔍𝔫𝔱𝔢𝔯𝔩𝔲𝔡𝔢

BY

ROBERT BUCHANAN

" *Diabolus Hominum Salvator.*"

" *Est Diabolus in nobis !* "

" αὐτὸς γὰρ ὁ Σατανᾶς μετασχηματίζεται ἐις ἄγγελον Φωτός." 2 Cor. xi., 14.

LONDON:

ROBERT BUCHANAN,

AND ALL BOOKSELLERS.

T
ℓS

PRINTED BY THE NEW TEMPLE PRESS
17, GRANT ROAD ADDISCOMBE, CROYDON.

CONTENTS.

	PAGE
DEDICATION	vii
THE DEVIL'S CASE	1
EPILOGUE: THE LITANY DE PROFUNDIS	159

DEDICATION.

November, 1894

When the life-thread was spun
  From the blood in her breast,
She look'd on her Son,
  Smiled, and rock'd him to rest. . . .

How swift the Hours run
  From the East to the West !
Erect stood the Son,
  And the Mother was blest.

Of all Life had won
  Love like his seem'd the best :
He was still the dear Son
  She had rock'd on her breast !

Yet lo ! all is done !
  (T'was, O God, Thy behest !)
In his turn the gray Son
  Rocks the Mother to rest !

All is o'er, ere begun ! . . . .
  O my dearest and best,
Sleep in peace,—till thy Son
  Creepeth down to thy breast !

                    R. B.

THE DEVIL'S CASE.

NOW FOR THE FIRST TIME CORRECTLY STATED, AND DILIGENTLY VERSIFIED, AS

A BANK HOLIDAY INTERLUDE.

———

Please remember, Gentle Reader,
Not to judge me line by line :
Tho' I try to state it clearly,
'Tis the Devil's Case, not mine !

THE DEVIL'S CASE.

I.

Would you know how I, Buchanan,
Met the Devil here in London,
Chatted with him, interview'd him ?
Listen, then, and you shall hear !

Not in great heroic measures
Shall I sing on this occasion,
But in roguish rhymeless stanzas
Much esteem'd by Greeks and Germans.

Genius of the Greeks and Germans,
Lend me, then, your light trochaics,
Loose, an easy-fitting raiment
Fit to lounge in, as I sing !

B

For my perilous subject-matter
Mingled is of jest and earnest,
To be treated in a manner
Jaunty, free, yet philosophic ;

Bold it is,—you'll cease to doubt it,
When I once am fairly started !
Sad it is,—and yet its sadness
Trembles on the verge of laughter !

Other bards in days departed
Have (they tell us) met the Devil ;
Often I'm inclined to doubt it
Since they libel'd him so grossly.

No ! the fiends of their acquaintance
Were but small inferior Devils,
Feeble foolish masqueraders,
Tho' their talk was often clever ;

Tho' to other generations
They might seem appalling creatures,
Really they were not authentic,
Not the GREAT ORIGINAL !

For the first time, I assure you,
He, the real and only Devil,
Sick of being by poets libel'd,
Has to utterance condescended ;

Wherefore, I entreat you, Reader,
Listen to his explanations!
Judge with kindness and discretion
Interview'd and Interviewer !

I, the Interviewer, hated
Cordially by cliques and critics,
Rail'd at in a hundred journals
As a Scotchman lost and lorn ;

He, the Interview'd, for ages
Outlaw'd by the cliques of Heaven,
Who for ever and for ever
Roll the Log and praise the Lord !

I, the Interviewer, banish'd
From the Eden of the poets,
Where the stainless laurel-wearers
Wander innocent and nude;

He, the Interview'd, for ever
Boycotted by God Almighty,
Curst in leader-writer's thunder
By the great celestial *Times.*

Neither of us, I assure you,
Has been reasonably treated ;
Neither of us is so naughty
As the public prints assever.

Both began with warm approval
Of the Church and ruling classes';
I was praised by the *Spectator,*
He was orthodox and holy !

Both, alas ! have wholly fallen !
I, from gulfs of impious thinking,
See the Heav'n of Poetasters
Guarded still by Hutton's sword';

He, the greater, grander Devil,
Prowling in the outer darkness,
Sadly eyes the loaves and fishes
On the Thunderer's banquet-table.

Still, we keep as our possession
One thing even the Angels envy—
Power to stand erect, while cravens
Roll the Log and bend the knee ;

Power to feel and strength to suffer,
Will to fight for Freedom only,
Zeal to speak the truth within us,
While the slaves of Heaven are dumb.

But. . . your pardon, Gentle Reader !
I'm anticipating somewhat—
All impatient waits my Devil,
Swishing tail and grimly smiling :

What he *is*, himself shall tell you—
What he thinks, you soon shall gather,
When I say, the Judge saluting,
"I'm, my lud, for the Defendant !"

II.

Night lay o'er the Heath of Hampstead—
One by one the merry-makers,
Romping, mad, accordion-playing,
Beer-inspired, were trotting town-ward.

All that afternoon I'd wander'd
Mid the throng of Nymphs and Satyrs,—
Now at last the Bacchanalian
August holiday was over.

Sad my soul had been among them,
Envying their easy pleasures,
Since for many a month behind me
Wolf-like creditors had throng'd ;

Since my name and fame were lying
In the gutter of the journals,
While the laws of Earth and Heaven
Seemed one vast Receiving Order !

Bankrupt thus in fame and fortune,
Wearily I walk'd and ponder'd
On the lonely Heath of Hampstead,
In the silence of the Night. . . .

Gently, one by one, the azure
Lattices of Heaven blew open ;
Dimly, darkly, far above me,
God began to light His lamps :

Silent, still, a shadowy Presence
Felt not seen, the Old Lamplighter
Pass'd above my head, fulfilling
Feebly his appointed task.

How my spirit rose against Him !
How I curst His deaf-and-dumbness !
While, above me, twinkle-twinkle
Gleam'd those melancholy lights !

Far down westward, over Harrow,
Pensively the Moon was shining—
Opening her dark bed-curtains
With a wan and sleepy smile ;

Soft and cool a breeze was blowing
Like the Earth's own breath in slumber,
Falling on my fever'd eyelids
With a dewy sense of tears.

Night was there, and Night within me,
As with sad eyes gazing sky-ward
I beheld the bale-fires burning,
Multiplying, overhead !

III.

He who hath not turn'd already
From my rakish, rhymeless poem,
Seeking what the crowd loves better,—
Rhyme and tintinabulation,

May esteem me a blasphemer,
Just as I, at our first meeting,
To be presently recorded,
Thought my honest friend, the Devil !

He alone blasphemes who smothers
Truth his conscience bids him utter ;
Now-a-days, in Hell and London,
Truth, methinks, is sorely needed !

And (remember) I, Buchanan,
Spite of all my slips, have ever
Loath'd the foul materialistic
Serpent that surrounds the world. . .

In his autobiographic
Fragment, Stuart Mill assevers
That from infancy to manhood
He was never pious-minded ;

Never did his spirit falter
Into Brahmic meditation :
Quite enough for him to brood on
Was the moral side of Man.

Souls like that the Fates may fashion,
But I fail to comprehend them—
From the hour I first remember
I was gazing at the stars ;

I was wondering, I was dreaming,
Speculating and aspiring,—
Reaching hands and feeling backward
To the secret founts of Being.

All the gods were welcome to me !
All the heavens were wide and open !
All the dreams of all the Dreamers
In my heart's blood were pulsating !

Beautiful it was to wander
In a glad green world, beholding
Faith's celestial Jacob's Ladder
Rainbow'd out 'tween Earth and Heaven,

And upon it shining Angels,
Some descending, some ascending,
Golden hair'd, with rosy faces
Smiling on me as I walk'd.

Well, those happy days were over,
With the roses of the Maytime—
One by one my youth's illusions
Had been spirited away.

Ev'n as eyeless Samson labour'd
Wearily 'mong slaves at Gaza,
I had done my daily taskwork,
Blind and sad, yet not despairing ;

Spite of all my load of sorrows,
I was hoping, I was dreaming ;
Still, tho' all my gods had vanish'd,
Reaching empty arms to Heaven !

IV.

Bitterly, that night of August,
All my load of woes upon me,
Bare I witness 'gainst the Serpent
Who had made me see and know.

Far away the Sword was flaming
O'er the gates of Youth and Eden—
Never, never, should I enter
Those celestial Gates again !

And the Woman ? Somewhere yonder
She was sorrowing and sobbing—
Never, never, would we wander
Thro' the Garden, hand in hand !

Bitterly I cursed the Serpent !
Bitterly I cursed the Apple !
Honey in the mouth, but wormwood
In the stomach, being eaten !

Suddenly my soul grew conscious
Of dark forms that flitted near me:—
All the pallid Heath was peopled
With the shadows of the Dead;

Woeful shadows,—well I knew them !
Phantoms of the years departed—
Men and women, apparitions
Of the days when I was young !

Never one (and this was strangest !)
Cast a look upon me passing—
Some gazed downward, darkly dreaming,
Others look'd on vacancy ;

Lost they seemed in contemplation,
All unconscious of my presence—
Some were smiling, some were weeping,
All were hastening God knows where !

Well I knew one weary figure
Bending as beneath a burden,
Talking to himself, nor heeding
While I sob'd and murmur'd " Father ! "

And another, whitely shrouded,—
Thin and spectral were her features
Underneath her locks all golden
As her namesake's, the Madonna's ;

And another, tall and slender,
Bright-eyed like the star of morning,
Beauteous as that other David
When he sang to comfort Saul !

And another, bright-eyed also,
Tho' the years had snowed upon him—
('Twas but yesterday, my Roden,
That dear hand was clasp'd in mine !)

Shadows, phantoms, apparitions,
Heedless though I cried unto them,
Though my wounded heart was bleeding
For a look, a loving word ;

Shadows dead, yet omnipresent,
Wrapt in Death as in a garment,
Heedless of the living creature
Who implored their intercession,

Ant-like moved they, this way, that way,
Purposeful yet void of purpose
As the ants are, ever thronging
Busily, they know not whither.

Never one stretch'd hand unto me !
Never one would look upon me !
All alone I stood among them
With a void and aching heart.

Far away, the lights of London
Glimmer'd like a crimson crescent !
Far above, the lamps of Heaven
Flicker'd in the breath of God !

V.

Suddenly from out the darkness
Sprang the Moon, and thro' the trembling
Pools of azure softly swimming
Flooded Heaven with rippling rays.

Well I knew the Naked Goddess!
Many a midnight, there in London,
She had witch'd my sense with wonder,
Stirr'd my soul to pensive dreams!

In her light the Phantoms faded,
While the lonely Heath around me,
Lit as with a ghastly daylight,
Loom'd distinct against the sky. . . .

Even then I saw before me
Something, featured like a mortal,
Sitting silent in the moonlight
On a fallen wither'd tree.

Gnarl'd and knotted like the branches
Seem'd his form, yet bent and weary,—
Worn his features were, and wither'd,
And his hair was white as snow.

In his hands he held the paper
He was quietly perusing,
Glancing up at times and gazing
At the City far away.

Startled to perceive a mortal
Sitting in a place so lonely,
Wondering I paused and watch'd him,
And betimes my wonder grew :

Silent, heedless of my presence,
Sat he reading by the moonlight,
Clerically dress'd, bareheaded,
Spectacles upon his nose.

" 'Tis," I thought " some priest or parson,
Or some layman who, like Mawworm,
Feels ' a call to go a preaching,'
Yet what folly brings him *here ?* "

C

Nearer then I stole unto him,
Keen to know what he was reading—
When I saw that 'twas the latest
(Pink) edition of the *Star*.

Still he heeded not my presence,
Till I broke the gloomy silence,
Saying, "Friend, your sight is surely
Wondrous for a wight so old,

" Since by moonlight dim as this is
You can read your evening paper ?"
As I spake he gazed upon me,
Smiling, with uplifted eyes.

" Yes," he said, benignly nodding,
"I am blest with goodly eyesight,
Owing chiefly, like most blessings,
To a strictly moral life.

" In my sanctum, sir, you find me,
After weary hours of labour,
Glancing, to refresh my spirit,
At the doings of the day.

" Never globe of gold or crystal,
Used by any Necromancer,
Flash'd more wonders on the vision
Than the Newspaper I hold!

" Here, epitomis'd and pictured,
We behold the human Pageant,—
All the doings on this planet,
All the stress and strife of men ;

" Kings pass by with trains attendant,
Shadowy Armies follow ever,
Ghostly faces glimmer on us,—
Everywhere the Phantoms pass !

" Scenes of wonder and of terror,—
Fields of battle dimly looming,
Cain still slaughtering his brother,
Having cast his Altar down ;

" Parliaments in congress gather'd ;
Judges on their benches nodding,
While the tedious sleepy trial
Oozes darkly, slowly, on ;

" Then, the groups of famish'd creatures !
Then, the Pit's Mouth, fiercely flaming,
While the wild-eyed wives and mothers
Clamour round and shriek for aid !

" Of all Miracles the greatest
Is the Newspaper," he added—
" Daily, hourly, adumbrating
All the anarchy of Life ! "

" Adumbrating too," I answer'd,
" All life's wonder, all life's beauty—
Telling men of mighty causes,
Solemn issues, glorious deeds !

" Heroes pass across its mirror,
Angel-faces flash before us,
Eyes of countless Saints and Martyrs
Cast upon us looks of love.

" Still the Seer, the Priest, the Poet
Speak of God, and point to Heaven !
Still the Churches stand, proclaiming
Life is more than mere despair."

" Surely ! " said the quiet Stranger ;
Here, ev'n *here*, the Soul is shining ;
Still the pious leader-writer
Vaunts the government of God !

" Church and State, Sir, Queen and Country,
Party Rule and all its blessings,
Progress, Culture, Loaves and Fishes,
Still are potent in the Land !

" Shibboleths like these are precious
Ev'n though one devours another,
Though the shibboleth of white men
Wrecks the shibboleth of black !

" Yet (you warn me) still the Dreamers
Speak of God and point to Heaven !
Still the spire, like Faith's bright finger,
Points to some far Paradise !

" Meantime, God is busy, bungling
In the old familiar fashion,
Heedless of the things He crushes
Underneath His clumsy foot !

VI.

" Take my Newspaper a moment ! "
(Here I did so) " Read the headings : "
" *Shipwreck of the Golden Mary—*
Loss of every Soul on board !

" *Earthquake in Sardinia.   Twenty*
Villages destroyed entirely.
Many thousand living creatures
Swallow'd in the black abysses. . . .

" *Floods in China . . . Decimation*
Of much populated districts,
Whither, while the folk were sleeping,
Rush'd the great destroying waters . . .

" *Cholera in Russia ! . . . Famine . . .*
In the East ! and millions starving ! . . .
Railway accident in Texas,
Sickening details " (columns long).

" Look on Nature.   Hear the wailing
Of a million martyr'd beings—
Tell me, then, the God you pray to
Cares one straw for human life !

" Well it is for *you*, sir, coming
From a fireside calm and cosy,
To believe some kindly Person
Rules the destinies of Earth !

" Pestilence, Disease, and Famine
Desolate this world you praise so ;
Who shall bid them cease their ravage ?—
Who shall say to Death—' go by !' "

Then I answer'd, hot and angry,
" Grant the pain and grant the carnage
(How my soul has sickened o'er them !)
Grant the thousand woes of men !

" This they prove, and this thing only :
Human life as we behold it
Is as nothing in the vision
Of a larger Thought than ours.

" All this world and its delusions,
All this life, its joys and sorrows,
Death itself, become as nothing,
When we learn that *nought* can die."

" Dreamer ! " said he, " One thing certain
Is the death of every unit :
Life, I grant you, is eternal,
But the personal life must pass.

" Nay, not only lesser beings,
But the greater with the lesser—
Like the individual unit
Dies the individual world !

" Look at men.   Regard them closely—
Mark the madmen chasing bubbles,
Pleasure, honour, reputation,
Gold and women most of all !

" Think you things like these are worthy
Of eternal prolongation ?—
God knows better—in Death's furnace
Melts the dross for other uses ! "

" God ? " he cried, " If such a Ruler,
Wise, Omnipotent, All-seeing,
Had concerned Himself in making
Worlds at all, and living creatures,

" He'd have made them wholly perfect,
With no fuss of evolution . . . ;
If there *is* a God, He blundered,—
Man is here to set Him right ! "

VII.

Horrified to hear such language
From a man so old and saintly,
" Sir," I said, " At first I took you
For a clergyman, or priest ?

" Now I hear you thus blaspheming,
I conclude that you're no parson—
Mother Church perchance has thrust you
Scornfully beyond its doors ? "

" Sir," he said, " your guess is clever !
Once I was in holy orders
(Long ago) and for my blunders
Heaven's Archbishop kick'd me out !

" Since that time, Sir, I've been busy
Prowling up and down your planet,
Whence I've come to this conclusion—
All Religion is a Fraud ! "

Like a spectacled Magician
Rose the man as he proceeded,
Blinking calmly down upon me
'Thro his glasses, with a smile ;

Tall and lean he tower'd above me,
Looming 'gainst the moonlit heaven,
Baleful rays of something evil
Glimmering from his rheumy eyes.

" Yes," he mutter'd, gazing upward;
" Though the stars may shine their brightest,
Though the Churches shriek their loudest,
God is utterly played out ! "

" Blasphemy ! " I cried, " Our Maker
Is, and works in His own fashion :
How shall purblind human creatures
Comprehend his works and laws?

" Shall ephemeræ of a moment,
Fluttering for a breath, then fading,
Fathom the Eternal Glory
Of the loving Lord of all?

" What we see of sin and sorrow
Is but darkness of the vision—
Far beyond it God the Father
Moveth to some fair Event !

" In due season those who love Him
Shall awake to understanding—
Meantime, certain of His wisdom,
Patiently they watch and wait ! "

" So they tell us in the Churches,"
Said the Stranger ; " so the Human,
Blindly hoping and despairing,
Postulates a God of Love !

" Since the world appears so evil,
It must surely be delusion !
So they argue in a circle,
Proving blindly, black is white !

" All the while their great Creator,
Moving to the Event you speak of,
Freely scatters his damnation
On two-thirds of living things !

' Let the Preacher and the Poet
Dream the old sweet dream of Heaven ;
Meantime, God reminds them daily
Of a warmer place below !

" Read my Newspaper ! the journal
Of the Inferno He created !
Tir'd of that, peruse the pages
Mark'd by History's bloody hand !

" Sheol burnt from the beginning,
Sheol burns to-day around us—
Countless millions of you mortals
Fail to feed its hungry fires !

" City still has followed City
Down this crater of damnation—
Still it yawns,—and o'er it London
Smokes, like Babylon of old !

" Here and there, from Hell and Chaos,
Some fair type is seen emerging—
Pleased to find his work so pretty,
God approves it for a space ;

" Then, dissatisfied and peevish,
Crushes it with foot or fingers !
Greece, Rome, Egypt, thus have perish'd,
Yet the fires of Hell burn on ! "

VIII.

Wroth to hear him still blaspheming,
Pitying, ne'ertheless, his blindness,
Since the years had snow'd upon him
And his face lookt worn and weary,

" Thinkest thou," I cried, " the Father,
Wise, omnipotent, all-seeing,
Ever would consign His children
To an anguish everlasting?

" Nay, there is no Hell, save only
Conscience working deep within us,
Warning us 'gainst sin and evil,
Ever whispering ' Repent!' "

Smiling quietly, the Stranger
Answer'd, " Sin is *God's* invention!
Often have I doubted Heaven—
Never have I doubted Hell!

" Look around.   Hell *is*.   Of all things
Made by God, the one thing certain."
Then with twinkling eyes he added,
" Just as soon, I'd doubt the Devil ! "

Lost in utter indignation
Scornfully I turned upon him :
" Cease thy blasphemy !   No magic
Can recall the Prince of Evil !

" Nay ! for Man has passed for ever
From those caves of superstition
Where that image cloven-footed
Of our sin was first created.

" Hell is *not*,—nor any Spirit
Wholly lost and wholly evil.
He who dares believe in either
Out of ignorance blasphemes."

" Pardon me," he smiling answer'd—
" What was done by old Magicians
Still is easy—Modern magic
Still is potent, be assured !

" Think of all the woes of Nature !
Picture, then, the Prince of Evil,
As thy conscience can conceive him—
Straightway he shall stand before you !

Yet I warn you, you may find him
Neither tail'd nor cloven-footed—
Nay, a person civil-spoken,
And extremely sympathetic ! "

Even as he spake, his features
Shone with vitreous rays reflected
From the heavens above him bending,
And his eyes grew bright as stars ;

And meseem'd his form dilated
As with soot-black wings, expanding
Into something strange and baleful,
Shadowy, mystical, and sad.

Like some ragged ancient raven
Stood he fluttering before me,—
While the moonlight's tremulous fingers
Smooth'd his woeful hoary hair !

D

Straightway, then, methought I knew him,
Shrinking back in trepidation,
Crying " Get behind me, SATAN ! "
Trembling in the act to fly !

IX.

" Stay," he said, " and listen to me !
I am he thy conscience pictures,
I am he whom men deem evil,
Anti-Christ and Anti-God !

" I have answer'd to thy summons !
I am he whom the Almighty,
Judge as well as prosecutor,
Ever hath condemn'd unheard.

" Never has the case been stated
Properly for the Defendant—
I entreat you, listen to me !
Set me right before the world !

" Purblind as the priests and prophets
Ev'n the Poets have traduced me,—
Ev'n the Poets, tho' I love them,
And have taught them all they know !

" Marlowe, tho' my favourite pupil,
Painted me a very Monster,
Corybantic, cloven-footed,
Insolent and goggle-eyed.

" Milton's Devil was a parson
Voluble and bellows-winded,
Like his garrulous God Almighty
Quite impossibly absurd.

" Calderon malign'd me also!
Painting in his assonantic
Magico Prodigioso
Only hideousness divine.

" All the others, down to Goethe,
Fed the foolish superstition—
Goethe, that superior person,
Blunder'd also, like his betters.

" Byron (tho' I loved the fellow!
Tho' I gave him wingëd arrows
To destroy the swinish virtues
In the pigsties of King George!)

" Byron could not paint me truly,—
'Stead of gazing in the mirror,
Where he surely might have found me,
Fair of face though lame of foot,

" He proclaim'd a prosy Devil
Like the fiend of Bailey, mixing
Bad blank verse and metaphysics
In the same old fashion'd style !

" Even Burns, my prince of singers,
Nature's sky-lark render'd human,
Treated me with scornful pity,
Prayed that I might mend my ways !

" Never one has comprehended
My true nature and profession ;
Every one of these, my chosen,
Sped the hideous libel on.

" I'm the kindest hearted creature
In this Universe of Sorrows !
My affection for you mortals
Is the cause of all my woes !

" Listen, then—for *you're* a Poet,
Equal in your own opinion
To the best of all those others,
Tho' extremely little read ;

" Men, be sure, will never make you
Laureate in a Christian Country,—
Nay, the office is abolish'd
Since no Christian Bard survives :

" Be the Laureate of the Devil !
Justify his ways to mortals !
State the case for the Defendant
Spite the *Times* and spite the gods !

" I have watch'd and waited for you
Since you sang that Yuletide Carol,
Picturing the Jew immortal
Wailing vainly for a Father !

" From the darkest depths of Sheol
I was marking and applauding. . . .
Having sung the only Jesus,
Go and sing the only Devil !

" Do it straightway ! and for ever
I'll protect your reputation !
Long as I, the Devil, am reigning,
You shall honour'd be in Hell ! "

Half in jest and half in earnest
Spake the Devil, smiling slyly,—
And I answer'd " Sing *your* praises ?
Devil take me if I do ! "

X.

" With your wish, sir, or without it,
He *will* take you soon or later ! "
Said he laughing grimly ;—" Wherefore
Do him, pray, this friendly turn !

" I've a case which, rightly stated,
Must procure me an acquittal :
Yes, the case for the Defendant
Will astonish God Himself !

" God's my Judge, and cannot therefore
As a witness speak against me ;
God the Judge must be—the Jury
Men of science and discretion.

" When they call the roll, you'll challenge
All the slaves of superstition,—
Fashionable priests and poets,
And all military men ;

" Thieves and publishers and critics
Shall be warn'd from off the jury,—
Ev'n philosophers and pundits
Must be keenly scrutinized.

" Politicians, Whig and Tory,
Jewish, Christian, and Agnostic,
Must be challenged—they are liars
Both by practice and profession.

" Lastly, challenge all the prying
Members of the County Council—
Prurient things of all three sexes,
Loathing Liberty and Light.

" Well I know that I shall triumph,
Since against me, as chief witness,
That disreputable person,
Jesus Josephson, is summon'd.

" I shall prove that Witness surely
The supremest of impostors—
One whom no enlighten'd thinker
Can believe upon his oath ! "

As he spake, his wrinkled features
Shrivel'd up to hideous seeming,
And his eyes flash'd bright, flamboyant
With a fierce and baleful light.

" Devil ! " cried I, " Prince of Devils !
Devil verily by nature,
Peace ! Blaspheme not ! He thou namest
Is a star above thy head !

" Man or god, or both united,
He, the beautiful Redeemer,
Far transcends in power and pity
All the draff of humankind.

" True or false, his Dream has gladden'd
Millions of created beings ;
Man or god, his love hath vanquished
All things evil, even Death ! "

As I spake, that troubled Spirit
Changed again—his gaze grew gentle—
From his face the anger faded,
And his eyes were dim with tears.

" Yea," he said, " thou speakest truly !
He thou nam'st was good and holy—
Pardon, pardon, Son of Sorrow,
Well-belovéd, even by *me* !

" Even in thy worst delusions
Thou wast holy, thou wast loving,
Yea, thy heart was great and gracious,
Tho' thine eyes were very blind.

" Yea, and *thou*, too, wast an outcast !
All thy goodly Dream is over !
He who rules thy realm, my Jesus,
Never wore thy crown of thorns !

" Not of *thee*, but of that other
Who usurps thine earthly kingdom,
Spake I; not of *thee*, my Jesus,
But of him they name the Christ.

" Yet . . . forgive me . . . of thine error
Was this evil monster fashion'd :
Blindly, gently, didst thou blunder,
Out of pure excess of Love.

" Thus, perchance, of all Souls living
Least thy spirit comprehended
Him who sits beyond these vapours
Heedless of His own Creation."

Pale he stood, like one invoking
Some benign and awful Spirit ;
Then he sigh'd and softly smiling
Turn'd his wistful eyes on mine.

Long he spake, with accents human,
In his own self-exculpation ;
Till at last I comprehended
Meanings that at first seem'd dark.

Then, while on his pallid features
Flamed the alien lights of Heaven,
"Come!" he cried. "Hell's fires burn yonder!
Come and gaze upon my Kingdom ! "

In a moment I was lifted
High in air, and wildly clinging
To the fringe of his dark raiment,
Wafted to the silent City.

XI.

As the cold metallic Ocean
Swings and clangs around the drowning,
So the solid air around me
Swung, till sense and sight departed;

Dimly, darkly, I was conscious
That I floated swiftly onward,
Moving to a rhythmic motion
Like the beat of mighty pinions.

Suddenly, like one in slumber
Falling wildly till he wakens,
Down like lead I seem'd descending
Dizzily I knew not whither,

Till at last, I shriek'd and struggled
Blind and breathless, and awaken'd,
And beheld him standing by me
Pointing with a spectral finger.

" Look," he said. " The Hell thou doubtedst
Burns for evermore around thee—
Wheresoever human creatures
Wail in anguish, is my Kingdom ! "

Then, methought, the moonlit houses
Everywhere became transparent,
And I saw the shapes within them
Hopeless, aimless, and despairing :

Dead and dying ; woeful mothers
Wailing over afflicted children ;
Creatures hollow-eyed with famine
Toiling on from dark to dawn ;

Haggard faces from their pillows
Gazing, as the pale nurse flitted
On from bed to bed in silence,
Mid the night-light's ghostly gleam :

Shapes sin-bloated from the cradle
Thrown in heaps obscene together,
While from gulfs of desolation
Rose the sound of idiot laughter !

Under arches dark and dreadful
Lay the murder'd corpse still bleeding,
While the murderer stood and listen'd
Wildly, with uplifted hair.

Everywhere Disease and Famine
Held their ghastly midnight revel—
Even in the darken'd palace
Rose the moan, the lamentation.

Everywhere a spectral Angel
Moved, with terrible forefinger
Touching shapes that shrank in anguish
With the flame that burns for ever :

On the cheeks of men and women
Fell the mark of that dread finger,
Burning inward, while the vitals
Gnaw'd with hell-fire life-consuming.

Then I turn'd to him who led me
Thither, and behold ! his features
Misted were with tears of pity
Falling from his woeful eyes !

Not on me those eyes were gazing
But at something far above us ;
Not to me his lips were saying
" Lord, I loathe thy Works and *Thee !*

" Just such measure as the Father
Metes to His afflicted children,
Would I mete to Thee, the Father,
In the name of those I rule !

" Thou hast given me my kingdom,
I accept its crown of sorrow,
Scorning still to kneel and thank Thee,
Pulseless, null Omnipotence ! "

As I listen'd, horror seized me,
" Nay," I cried, to Heaven upgazing,
" Blame not Him who first created
All things beautiful and fair—

" He, the holy Heavenly Father,
Mourns the woe of things created—
Out of sin that woe was fashion'd,
And our sin arose from *thee* ! "

Pityingly he gazed upon me.
" Sin," he said, " was *God's* invention !
He created Hell, my kingdom,
Tho' I wear its earthly crown !

" I, the eternal Prince of Darkness,
Found it ready for my coming—
Pestilence, Disease, and Famine
Burnt there, by the will Divine !

" Since that hour of my accession
I, the Devil, have ruled benignly,
Seeking like a kindly monarch
To improve my woeful realm.

" Thus, in spite of the Almighty,
I have leaven'd its afflictions,
Teaching men the laws of Nature,—
Wisdom, Love, and Self-control.

" Every year the Hell-fires lessen,
Every day the load is lighten'd,
'Neath my care the very devils
Grow benign and civilized !

" This I have achieved entirely
By the very means forbidden
At the first by God Almighty,—
Teaching men to see and know.

" Prince of liars was the pedant
Who aver'd that man's afflictions
Came from eating that first apple
From the great Forbidden Tree!

" From its seeds, by *me* ungather'd,
Many a living tree hath sprouted—
Where those trees bear fruit, believe me,
Even Hell resembles Heaven!

" Whoso eats that fruit forbidden
Knows himself and finds salvation,
Stands erect before his Maker,
Claims his birth-right and is free.

" Thus, for ages after ages,
I, the Devil, have drain'd the marshes,
Cleansed the cesspools, taught the people,
Like a true Progressionist!

" By the living Soul within me
I have conquer'd !—tho' for ages
I have been most grossly libel'd
By the foolish race of mortals.

" All my errors have proceeded
From a sympathetic nature ;
Prince of Evil men have styled me,
Who alone am Prince of Pity !

" Never man-god, Christ or Buddha,
Ever anguish'd more sincerely
For the sufferings of others,
Than myself, whom men call Devil.

" What is further to my credit,
I'm not merely sentimental—
I have practically labour'd
To improve the world's affairs.

" I'm the father of all Science,—
Master-builder, stock-improver,
First authority on drainage,
Most renown'd in all the arts.

" While the Priests have built their Churches
To a God who does not heed them,
I have fashion'd decent dwellings,
Public hospitals, and baths.

" ' Take no heed about To-morrow,'
Said the man-God, ' do no labour,
Be content with endless praying
And eternal *laissez-faire.*'

" But the Devil, being wiser,
Knows that he who fails to reckon
With the morrow, will discover
That To-morrow is To-day !

" And To-day is, now and ever,
All Eternity or nothing—
He who sits and twiddles fingers
Now, hath done it evermore ! . . .

" From which statement you may gather
I, the Devil, am transcendental—
Wise in all the ways of knowledge
Even down to metaphysics.

" This I merely state *en passant,*
Lest you deem me uninstructed,—
All philosophers I've studied,
From Heraclitus to Hegel."

XII.

Once again I was uplifted
High in air, but now my spirit
Wing'd (methought) beside the Devil
Like a kestrel by an Eagle;

Strength and insight grew within me,
Tho' my heart was sick with sorrow,
As we hover'd for an instant
O'er the silent lamplit City!

Far beneath on lonely bridges
I beheld the outcast women,
Sisters sad of lust and midnight,
Wandering weary and forlorn.

Over palaces and prisons,
Over hospitals and brothels,
Wheresoever Hell is burning,
Flew I, wafted as on wings.

From the tainted founts of Being
I beheld the new-born rising,
Sick, sin-bloated scum of infants
Fashion'd out of shameful slime ;

What the dead men and the dying
Sow'd in shame these reaped in sorrow,—
Thick as bubbles on a cauldron
They were coming, breaking, going.

Over waters black with tempest,
Where the ships were lightning-riven,
Where the terror-stricken seamen,
Sinking, shrieked aloud to God !

Over plains where ghostly armies
Came and went, and smote each other,
While the priests from the high places
Cried them on, and waved the Cross ;

Over silent legions waiting
For the nod of moon-struck rulers ;
Over countries famine-smitten ;
Over cities foul with plague ;

Wheresoever Hell is burning
I was wafted !—From mine eyrie
I beheld the exiles crawling
To the black Siberian mine ;

Shrieks of men and wails of women
Fill'd the air with lamentation,
While the Cossack cold and silent
Plied the knout and join'd the chain.

I beheld the lonely Leper,
With his face to heaven uplifted
Blotted out of human likeness,
Crawling to his nameless grave.

I beheld the arméd Arab
Ravishing the black man's village ;
I beheld the red race dying
Dumbly, like a deer at bay.

Everywhere the strong man triumph'd !
Everywhere the weak lay smitten !
Everywhere the gifts of Godhead
Rain'd on over-laden hands !

Everywhere (and this was strangest)
Priests were praying, men were kneeling,
Everywhere the broken martyrs
Lifted piteous eyes to Heaven !

Wheresoever Hell is burning
I was wafted ! and the bale-fires,
Fed with human lives for ever,
Burnt from Europe to Cathay.

. . . Like strange forms reflected darkly
In the glass of a Magician,
Ever flitting, ever fading,
Gleam'd the ghastly shapes of Sheol !

Till my soul grew faint within me
And again the air around me,
Ev'n as seas around the drowning,
Swung, and sense and sight departed.

XIII.

. . . On the lonely Heath of Hampstead
I awaken'd, and beside me
Saw the woe-worn outcast standing,
Shadowy, mystical, and sad.

Even as I gazed upon him,
All the baleful hideous seeming,
Falling from him like a garment,
Left him beautiful and fair !

Lost in awe I gazed upon him !
Angel-naked stood the Devil ;
Thin and tall ; upon his forehead
Light, as of some dim grey Dawn !

Fair he seem'd, tho' pale and weary,
Sorrowful, but softly shining,
Beautiful, as when, ere fallen,
Seated on the morning star !

Not on me his eyes were gazing,
But upon the far-off City;
Not to me his lips were saying,
" Lord, I loathe thy Works and Thee!"

Once again that out-cast Angel
Turned his luminous eyes upon me,—
Dark deep eyes that seem'd to suffer
From the light they shed around them;

Rays as of the star of morning
Glimmer'd o'er him as he murmur'd
In a voice like stars vibrating:
" Thing of clay, dost know me *now* ? "

" Yea," I said, " immortal Spirit,
Now at last I seem to know thee,
And my spirit yearns in kinship
With thy beauty and thy woe!"

Once again he cast upon me
Luminous looks of scorn and pity:
As a trembling star's reflection
Shakes in shadowy shallow waters,

Fell the glory of the Angel
On the waters of my spirit,
While I trembled, half in terror,
Half in wondering adoration.

" Thou art He, the Prince of Evil,
Whom thy God created perfect,
Yet who, doubting and rebelling,
Sank to darkness and despair ?"

"Yea," he answer'd, darkly frowning,
" I am He thy conscience pictures !
Lucifer once named up yonder,
Satan now re-named, the Devil !

" At the elbow of the Father
Once I stood and sang His praises—
Endless praises and hosannahs
To the crownéd King of Heaven.

" So I could have sung for ever,
Drinking rapture from His presence :
In an evil hour I wander'd
From His side, to view Creation !

" And at first I sang the louder,
Marvelling at His works and wonders—
Suns and stars and constellations
Join'd my joyful hallelujah ! "

As he spake he seem'd to brighten,
Dazzling all my sense with wonder,—
Round about him like a raiment
Clung a cloud of golden music !

" Such I was, His servant-angel !
Such I was, and so I worshipt !
Then from out the worlds he fashion'd
Came a wail, a lamentation.

" On the sun I stood, down-gazing
O'er the universe around me,
And the wail grew shriller, louder,
Till my joyful song was drown'd.

" Far away, where'er my vision
Wander'd, I beheld his Angels
Watching for His lifted finger,
Now creating, now destroying ;

" Here a moaning world was shrivel'd
Like an infant in the cradle;
Here a planet shrank in darkness
To a sound of souls despairing;

" Everywhere across Creation
Were the threads of Being broken,
Everywhere the Lord Almighty
Crush'd like shells the worlds He made !

" Then my soul was wroth within me,
And I cried to the Almighty:
' Evil, Lord, is Thy creation,
Since Thou sufferest pain to be !

" ' Or if pity stirs within Thee
For the woes of Thy creating,
Thou art even as Thine Angels
Strong, but not Omnipotent !

" ' Back on Thine own footsteps treading,
Ever slaying and re-making,
Ever bungling, Thou art only
Demigod, not God at best ! '

" Then He struck me with His lightnings,
Me, and many lesser angels,
Who in pity and compassion
Echo'd my protesting cry ;

" Smitten here upon the forehead,
Down I fell thro' the abysses,
Clinging wildly for a moment
To some star, as to a straw !

" Till I reached this lonely planet,
Stood upon it, and before me
Saw the naked Pair in Eden
Praising Him, as *I* had done.

" Tempt them, try them, undeceive them ! "
Said the Father's voice from Heaven—
" But be sure that deeper knowledge
Only means more swift despair ! "

" For a space I hesitated,
Seeing them so blindly happy,
Even as the beasts that perish
Knowing naught of Time or Death ;

" Then I said (may Man forgive me !)
Better far to know and suffer,
Reach the stature of us angels,
Than be happy like the beasts.

" Wherefore, as thou know'st, I tempted
First the Woman, whispering to her,
While she munch'd the golden apple,
Hints of nakedness and shame.

" Then I saw the Pair forthdriven
From the golden Gates of Eden,
Hunted, while I wept for pity,
By the bloodhound-angel, Death ! "

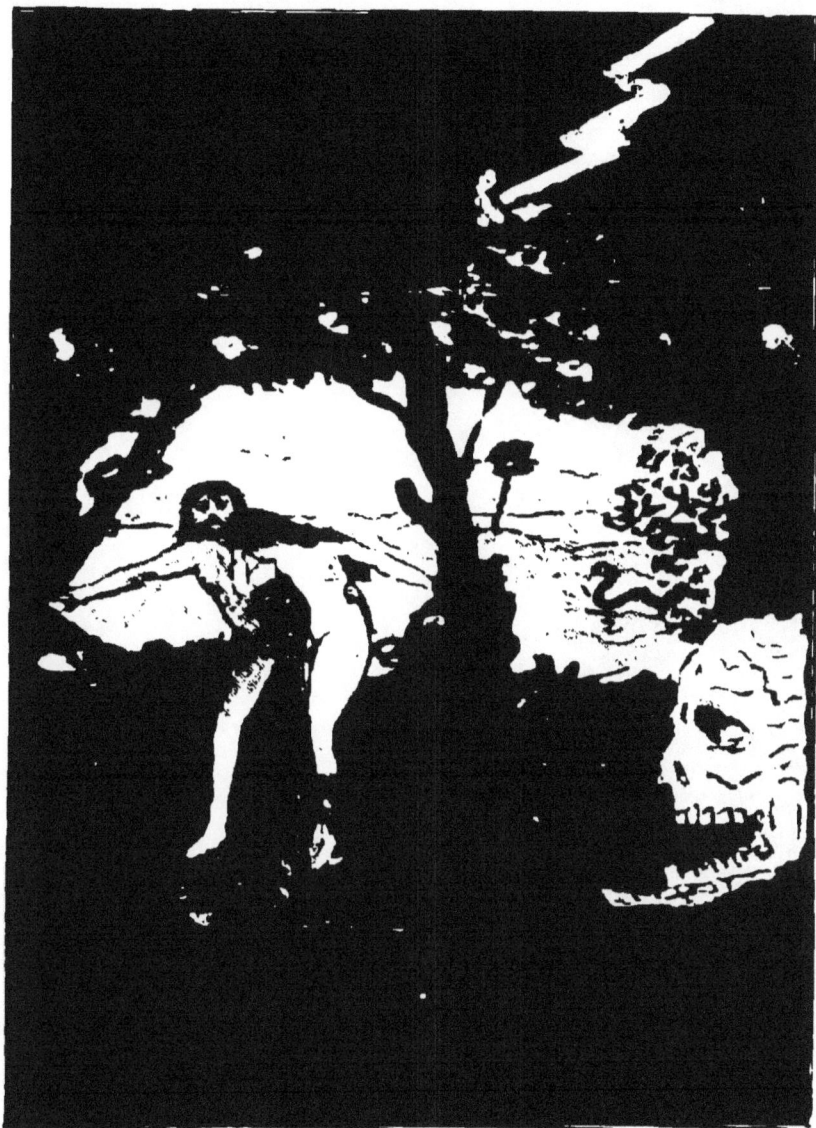

"THEN I SAW THE PAIR FORTH DRIVEN."

Page 64.

XIV.

While he spake his starry splendour
Faded, ever growing dimmer,—
Sadder, darker, stood the Angel,
Fixing weary eyes on mine ;

Clouds of woe were gather'd round him
Ev'n as raiment, and upon them
Silvern tremors caught the moonlight,
Glimmering like the Serpent's coils.

" Forth the Exiles fled together,
Knowing not of that dread Angel
Ever following their footsteps
Thro' their weary wanderings ;

" From the woman's womb there blossom'd
Little children, and their voices
Fill'd the solitude with music,
While the parents toil'd and gladden'd ;

F

"And the world grew green about them,
God and Eden were forgotten,
Till the Father's voice from Heaven
Cried for prayers and adulation ;

" Till that hour of desolation
When the first-born smote his brother,—
And upon him, from the shadows,
Sprang the pallid bloodhound, Death !

" Then they heard a voice above them
Thundering ' Out of sin and sorrow,
Thro' that fruit by Me forbidden,
Death is brought into the world ! '

" I, the Sapient Snake, knew better !
I, the Outcast, deeply lesson'd
In the book of God's Creation,
Knew the Heavenly Voice was *lying !*"

As he spake his shape grew shrunken
Into something black and baleful,
Woefully his eyes were burning
Like the eyeballs of the Serpent.

" Death was born in the beginning
By the will of God the Father ;
Ever slaying and destroying
Death had crept from world to world !

" Thro' the Universe were scatter'd
Shrouded spheres that once were living ;
Everywhere in yonder heavens
Life had broken like a bubble !

" Nay, this very world of Eden
Was a Sepulchre ; within it
Countless races long forgotten,
Slain of old by Death, were sleeping.

" Blindly, feebly, God had blunder'd,
Type on type had been rejected,
Race on race had come and vanish'd,
Ere the Human flowered in Adam.

" From the throats of things created
Wails of anguish had arisen,
Since above the waste of waters
Wingéd flew the pterodactyl.

" In the rocks and 'neath the Ocean
Lay the bones of beasts and monsters ;
Ages ere the Pair was fashioned,
Human-featured walk'd the Ape.

" Nay, the very Pair I tempted
Were no separate creation,—
Their perfection had proceeded
From a long ancestral line ;

" Ages ere their evolution
God had bungled, God had blunder'd,—
Now selecting, now rejecting,
Harking back, and retrogressing ;

" Thus the Archetype was fashion'd
Thro' perpetual vivisection,—
Countless swarms of martyr'd creatures
Mark'd his passage to the Human.

" This I knew, and this I purposed
Teaching long ago to mortals,—
But for many an age of darkness
Mortals mourn'd, but would not listen.

" While the tribes and generations
Multiplied from father Adam,
O'er the world in which I wander'd
Spread the Pestilence, Religion.

" Nations, Jacob's seed and Esau's,
White and red and particolour'd,
Rose, and in the desert places
Swarm'd the soot black seed of Ham.

" Busy still in every City,
Under every tent and dwelling,
Death abode, and never tiring
Did the bidding of his Master.

" Then in every Nation, shadow'd
With the darkness pestilential,
Priests arose, and woeful altars
Steam'd with sacrifice to God.

XV.

" Meantime I, the Accurst, was busy !
Whensoe'er I spake with mortals
Men grew gentle to each other,
While I taught them peaceful arts :

" How to till the soil, to fashion
Roofs of stone against the tempest,
How to weave the wool for raiment,
Yoke the monsters of the field ;

" Fire I brought them,—teaching also
How to tame it to their uses,—
Turning ironstone to iron,
Frame the ploughshare and the sword ;

" Help'd by me they drain'd the marshes,
Lop'd the forest trees, and fashion'd
Ships that floating on the waters
Gather'd harvest from the Deep.

" Bravely would my work have thriven,
Save for cunning Priests and Prophets,
Who, by dreams of God inflated,
Blunder'd ever like their Master. . . .

Yonder by the yellow Ganges
Rose the Temples of the Brahmin,—
Threefold there the mystic godhead,
Agni, Indra, Surya, reign'd.

" By the impassive, cruel features
Well I recognised the Father,—
Huge as some primaeval monster
Crawl'd He in the Vedic ooze.

" Mystical, uncomprehended,
In their shadowy shrines He brooded,
Silent, and the souls of mortals
Crawl'd like fearful snakes before Him.

" Thither, serpent-wise, I follow'd,
Whispering ' Strange is God and mighty;
Yet, altho' He fashion'd all things,
Impotent in utter godhead.'

" With my gospel pantheistic
I perplex'd their Priests and Prophets,
Tho' in spite of all my teaching,
Still they pray'd, and preach'd, and fasted.

" Still the cloud of superstition
Darken'd Earth and shrouded Heaven,
While the shivering naked people
Trembled at the priestly thunder. . . .

" Further East I wing'd, and burning
Like a sunbeam from the zenith,
On a sunlit mountain summit
Found the Persian, Zoroaster.

" Crying, 'If thou needs must worship
What transcends thine understanding,
Raise thine eyes, behold the Fountain
Whence the Light of Life is flowing!

" Him I left upon his mountain,
Crimson fires of dawn around Him—
Gazing till his eyes were blinded
At his Sun-god, and adoring. . . .

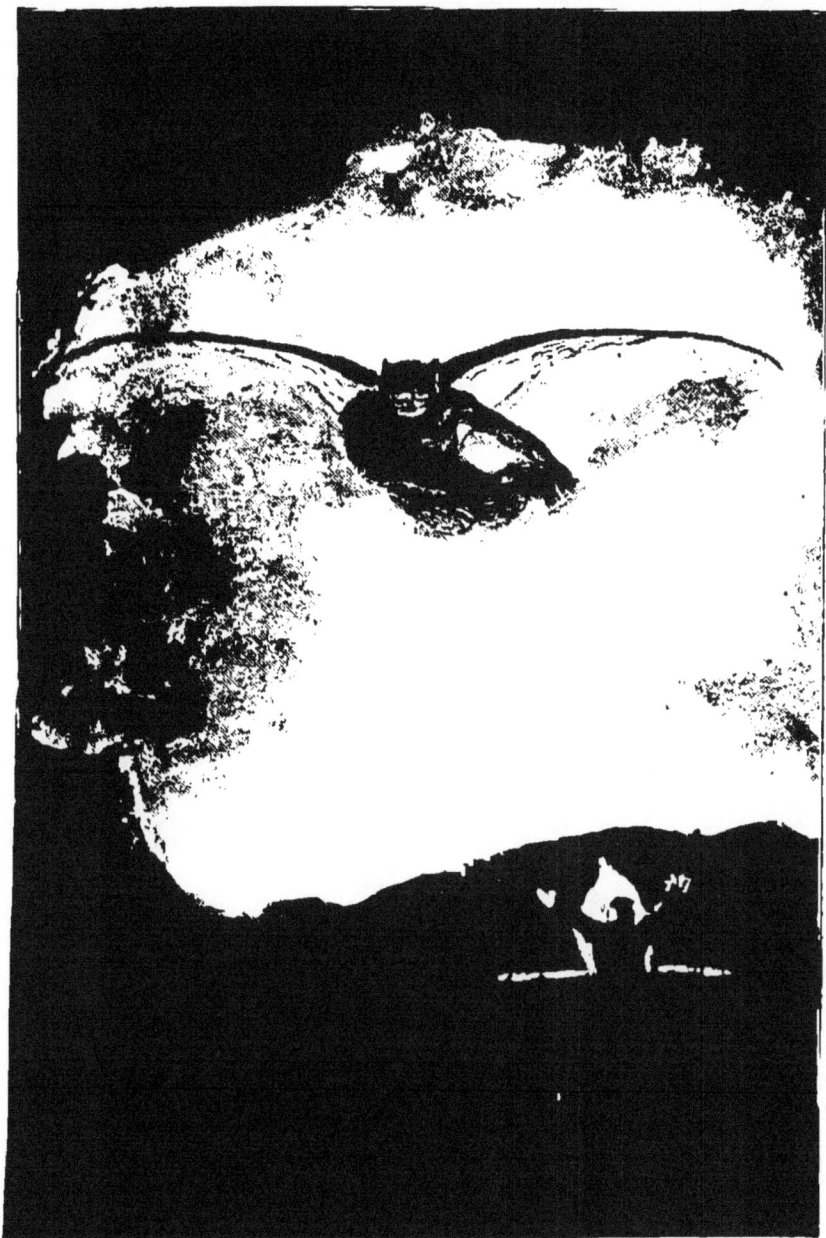

"FOUND THE PERSIAN, ZOROASTER."

" On the threshold of his palace
Stood the monarch Arddha Chiddi,
Roseate robes of youth were round him,
Yet his eyes were full of sorrow ;

" Down beneath him on the river
Corpses foul of men and women
Floated seaward, gnaw'd and eaten
By the watersnakes and fishes.

" Him I spake with, sadly showing
Death alone was lord and master
Over all the worlds created,
And that Death was surely evil.

" Never since the world's beginning,
Throb'd a human heart more gentle—
In its secret fount of sorrow
Stir'd the living springs of pity :

" From his palace door he wander'd,
Left the pomps of power behind him,
Wrapt a linen shroud about him,
Weeping for the woes of mortals.

" Yet, in spite of all my teaching,—
How to snatch from Death and Sorrow
Strength to live and zeal to labour,
In despite of God the Father,—

" He, the Buddha, sought oblution
In the waters of Nirwâna,
Crying loud ' There is no Father—
Only Death and Change for ever ! '

" Thus, denying God, he enter'd
God's great darkness of Negation,
Till the living springs of pity
Froze at last to calm despair ;

" Till, denying yet believing,
Conquering yet by godhead conquer'd,
He to Death as Lord and Master
Bow'd the saintly head, and blest him !

" Countless swarms of living creatures
Follow'd him into the darkness,—
White and wondrous o'er his kingdom,
Rose the Temples of the Lama ;

" Countless millions still despairing
In his temples gather kneeling—
Priests of Lama, blindly praying,
Swing the piteous lamps of Death.

" Thus the first and best of mortals
Conquer'd was, and o'er my Buddha
Brooded still the joyless, deathless,
Impotent Omnipotence ! ...   -   .

XVI.

" High in air on eagle-pinions
I, the outcast Angel, hover'd—
Gazing sadly down while mortals,
Ants on ant-hills, toil'd and struggled.

" Here and there were arméd nations
Moving restless hither and thither ;
'Mong the mountains, gazing upward,
Gather'd lonely tribes of shepherds.

" Ever darkly multiplying,
Crowning Kings and hailing prophets,
Toiling blindly in the darkness,
Grew the races of the Human.

" Ever 'mong them Death was busy,
Evermore the units perish'd,
Evermore the newborn creatures
Swarm'd from out the depths of Being.

" Nought they knew of Heaven above them,
Nought of Earth itself, their dwelling,
Circling with the mightier planets
Round the heliocentric fires ;

" Everywhere the Priest was busy
Raising temples, building altars,—
Everywhere the foolish Prophets
Raved aloud and wail'd for wonders ;

" Everywhere the martyr'd peoples
Toil'd and struggled and were smitten,
Evermore, to blind their senses,
Signs and miracles were wrought.

" Mong the people rose Messiahs,
Preaching, healing, prophesying,—
Pointing to the empty heavens
With a wan and witless smile. . . .

" By the Nile the son of Isis
Walked and mused,—upon his mantle
Mystic signs were wrought in silver,
And he wore a crown of thorns,—

"Saying ' Lo, from Phthah the Maker,
I, the human Emanation,
Come, and I elect to suffer,
To appease His righteous anger.'

Then the people sprang upon him,
Stript him bare and crucified him—
Pityingly I bent above him,
As he swung upon his Cross.

" Then the faithful who revered him,
In their spicy clothes embalmed him,
While the priesthood which had slain him
Hail'd him ' Son of God, Osiris ! ' "

" 'Mong his worshippers I lighted,
Priestly raiment wrapt around me,
Crying with them, ' Hail, Osiris !
Woman-born and yet divine ! '

" ' Kingly men and mighty monarchs
Are indeed the only godhead—
Wherefore let them have our praises,
Endless worhip and hosannahs.'

"HAIL, OSIRIS!
WOMAN-BORN, AND YET DIVINE!"

Page 78.

" Then I taught them hieroglyphics,
Mystic shapes and signs and letters,
Where the story of the Ages
Written was on brass and stone ;

" Then the busy Ants of Egypt
Raised the Pyramids ; around them
Shaping colonnades and pylons
For the sepulchres of Kings.

" Thus I taught them architecture,—
How to hew the rocks and fashion
Monuments that stand for ever
In despite of God and Time.

" Nay, to mock the mute Almighty,
I the mystic Sphynx invented,
Silent, impotent, impassive,
Gazing on a million graves !

" Numbers, too, I taught the people,—
How to measure Earth and Water,
By the stars and their progressions
Guide the floods and count the seasons.

" Then the God I had offended
Spread his darkness over Egypt,
Sent his Angels, hither, thither,
Turning men against each other ;

" While the haggard Priests and Prophets
Wail'd and work'd their signs and wonders,
The Assyrian and Egyptian
Struggled in their death-embraces.

" Vain was all that I had taught them—
Peace and wisdom, light and knowledge,
Strength to raise in spite of Nature
Pyramids of mortal making,—

" 'Gainst the angels masquerading
In the forms of Gods and Demons,
Shrieking loud from blood-stain'd altars
For their holocausts of Death.

" Pharoahs came and Pharoahs vanish'd,
Cities rose and Cities perish'd,—
Still arose, o'er seas of slaughter,
Those sad Sphynxes I had fashion'd. . . .

XVII.

" Far away, 'mong sea-girt islands
Dwelt a race of blue-eyed mortals—
From the happy groves of Hellas
Rose the lyric song of shepherds.

" Knowing nought of God the Father,
Innocent they were and happy,—
Merrily they piped, and round them
Danced my Satyrs and my Fauns.

" I, too, went and dwelt among them,
Gentle, wise, yet cloven footed,—
Fruit and flowers they brought, and gladly
Hail'd me as the wood-god, Pan."

While he spake his face grew gentle
As the shadows on the greensward,
From his throat came woodland music
Heard in Arcady of old.

G

" Taught by me they loved and welcomed
All the living powers of Nature—
Every tree was sweet and human,
Every fountain was a goddess.

" From the turquoise seas I summon'd
Aphrodité fair and naked---
Side by side we sang, and lovers
Gather'd hand in hand to listen.

" Fairer than the long lost Eden
Seem'd the sea-girt land of shepherds,—
Never tree of fruit forbidden
Grew within the groves of Faunus.

" Suddenly the heavens above us
Darken'd, spirits passed in thunder,—
From the far Caucasian mountains
Came a cry of lamentation.

" Swift as light I travelled thither
Over waters torn with tempest;—
Nail'd unto a rock and bleeding
Hung Prometheus Purkaeus !

" While the vulture tore his entrails
Not a sound the Titan utter'd,
But beneath the Cross lamenting
Gather'd woeful wailing women.

" Of my flesh this Christ was fashion'd,
From the side of me, the Devil,
He was born in the beginning,
Ev'n as Eve was born of Adam !

" On his calm undaunted spirit
Fell my heritage of sorrow—
Love for men, eternal pity
For the lot of living creatures.

" Then I knew that God was waking
From his stupor of inaction ;
Darkly out of yonder heaven
Gazed the silent sphynx-like Face ! . . .

" Taught by him, the mighty Titan,
Men had built a marble City,
Athens,—on the heights above it
Stood the snow-white Parthenon ;

" In the streets and groves of Athens
Calmly walk'd the seers and sages,
Words of wisdom dropped like honey
From the mouths of mighty teachers ;

" Harp in hand went happy poets
With their singing robes about them,
Music as of birds and fountains,
Mingling sweetly, fill'd the air.

" Here, ev'n here, despite the Titan,.
Priests of God and Death were busy :
In the Temples knelt the people
Seeking woeful signs and omens ;

" There the image of Athené
Blink'd her eyes, and idols sweated,
While the Augurs, bloody-finger'd.
Read the entrails of the slain.

" Then to many a mighty poet
I unfolded Nature's riddles :
Aeschylos, my word-compeller,
Sang the Titan's martyrdom !

" Vain was all my loving labour !
Tho' I lavish'd gifts upon them,
Tho' to witch their eyes with beauty
Phidias breathed his soul through stone,

" Tho' the poets and the sages
Spread my peace and benediction,
Tho' the laws of Earth and Heaven
Sifted were by gentle seers,

" Still the Priests of Heaven against me
Smote with all the strength of godhead,
Still the people, crouching dumbly,
Moan'd for miracles and signs.

" Vain was all my strife for mortals !
Vainly wrought my servant-angels !
Vainly toil'd Asclepios, vainly
Helen smiled, and Sappho sang !

" As a rainbow dies from Heaven,
As a snow-white cloud of summer
Breaks and fades, the pride of Hellas
Brighten'd, melted, past away ! "

XVIII.

Piteously the stars of Heaven
Fix'd their million eyes upon him,—
While his dark form droopt, and slowly
Darken'd, like a blackening brand ;

Brightness of the Angel faded
Into darkness sad and baleful,—
Old at last he seem'd and human,
Bending 'neath the load of years ;

In his voice I heard no longer
Music as of stars vibrating,
Sound of solemn psalms, or pipings
Of the merry flocks of Pan ;

Nay, the voice that spake unto me
Broken seem'd, like chimes discordant
Ringing over lonely uplands
In the silence of the night.

"Thus," he said, " the light of Hellas
Died away in desolation,
Setting where it first had risen
'Mong the eastern pyramids !

" O'er the land of seers and poets
Blew the breath of God's dark Angel,
Broken lay the marble statues
Of my tutelary gods !

" Meantime, like another Titan,
Rome had risen !—Strong and mighty,
From the mountains swarm'd the savage
Tribes of Romulus the shepherd.

" 'Mong them walk'd my servant-angels
Teaching them the lore of Nature,—
Strong they grew and ever stronger
Till they conquered Earth and Sea.

" Earth and Sea I gave unto them,
Saying, ' Surely ye are strongest !
Since no tyrants dwell among you,
Since ye know not fraud or fear ! '

" Tutelary gods I gave them,
Harmless gods whom they might worship,
Since I knew that in His creatures
God had sown the lust of godhead ;

" Strong they grew and ever stronger,
Building thus their great Republic,—
Fair and great it rose, and o'er it
All the winds of plenty blew.

" Then, to mar my work forever,
God the Eternal Tyrant fashion'd
Lesser tyrants in His image,—
So His Cæsars rose, and reign'd !

"'God's they were, not mine, the Devil's !
Nay, by Hades, I abjure them !
Freedom comes of Light and Knowledge,
Tyranny is born of God !

" Ever, since the world's beginning,
I, the gentle Prince of Pity,
Taught one Trinity to mortals—
Wisdom, Love, and Self-control—

" ' Shed no blood, since God doth shed it !
Love each other, help each other,
Rise erect against all tyrants,'
Is my gospel evermore.

" ' Only for a little season
Shalt thou draw the breath of Being—
Try to make that little season
Bright and glad, in spite of God ! '

" Turn the records of the Roman !
Read again the blood-stain'd pages !
See the spectres of the Cæsars
Passing on to endless night !

" Nay, but even here *I* triumph'd !
From the cesspool and the palace
Rose the cry of slaves and tyrants
Saying ' Death alone is God ! '

" So the crown of God descended
On the brows of Death, his angel !
So the Tyrant of Creation
Found no worshippers at last !

" Then, as in the eternal City
I was wandering weary-hearted,
Outcast from the hideous revels
Where the crownéd Spectre reign'd,

" Sick of God and God's creation,
I, the Devil, heard the crying
Of a voice amid the Desert,—
Saying, ' Rejoice, the Christ is born ! '

" Eastward flew I, and I found Him,
Best and worst of the Messiahs,
Walking meekly, meditating,
By the Lake of Galilee ! "

"BY THE LAKE OF GALILEE."

Page 90.

XIX.

For a space his voice was silent—
In his hands his face was buried,
While the elemental Darkness
Clung about him like a cloud ;

Wonderingly I gazed upon him,
For I knew that he was weeping—
Till, at last, again I saw him
Pointing angrily to Heaven.

Woefully, with snake-like glimmers,
Clung the coils of his black raiment,
Scornfully he laugh'd, and round him
Glimmer'd with a serpent's eyes.

"Let Him rise, and keep his promise!
Let Him wake, who sleeps for ever !
King of poets and of dreamers
Was this moon-struck Son of God!

" Him I fronted in the desert,
Pointing out his mad delusion,—
Fool, he wrapt his rags about him,—
" Σατανᾶ, ὀπίσω μου ! '

" Feeble, gentle, Thaumaturgist !
What knew *he* of God the Father ?
Pityingly I bent above him
As he swung upon the Cross !

" Yea, and blest him, little knowing
How the seed of his delusion,
Sown in love and human kindness,
Should be reap'd on fields of blood.

" I, the Devil, as they style me,
Have dispensed a benediction !
He, the Christ, self-styled, self-chosen,
Has become a wingéd curse !

" Dead, his crown of thorns beside him,
In his sepulchre he slumbers,—
Dust to dust, ashes to ashes,
Never can he wake again !

" Yet the lies his folly father'd
Live and multiply above him :
Lie the First ! ' A life hereafter
Shall redeem the wrongs of this ! '

" *Lie the Second !* ' Love thy neighbour
As thyself ! ' The dream, the fancy !
Were it true, each soul's existence
Would be proved by self-negation.

" *Lie the Third !* ' About the morrow
Take no heed—sufficient ever
Is the evil of the moment—
Take no trouble to redress it ! '

" *Lie the Fourth !*—' Lord God the Father
Loves his children and redeems them '—
He ?—the loveless, pulseless, deathless,
Impotent Omnipotence !

" Well, he staked his life, and lost it !
Flock on flock of sheep have follow'd
That bell-wether of the masses
Into darkness and despair !

" Eighteen hundred years of Europe
Have been wasted spite my warning :
' Fools, one life is all God grants you,
Sweep your houses, heed your drains !

" 'Love each other, help each other,
Juggle not with dreams and phrases—
Make ephemeral existence
Beautiful, in spite of God !

" ' Pass from knowledge on to knowledge
Ever higher and supremer,
Clothe these bones with power and pity,
Live and love, altho' ye die !

" ' Fear not, love not, and revere not
What transcends your understanding !
Keep your reverence and affection
For the brethren whom ye know !'

" Fools, they heard but did not heed me !
Far away from 'mong the vapours
Came the sound of their bell-wether
Tinkling to the same old tune !

" While the poets, priests and prophets
Gather'd, crying ' Listen ! listen ! '
To the church-bells' ululation
Rose the Christian holocaust !

" While the haggard priests and prophets
Pray'd aloud and cried for wonders,
Christs of Cyprus and Tyana
Heal'd the sick and raised the dead.

" God had conquered, with his darkness
Blotting out my stars of promise ;
Three times to the mad Plotinus
He revealed his sphinx-like features.

" God had conquer'd, Death was reigning
O'er the lands of Light and Morning ;
Plato's music turned to discord
In the mouth of Porphyry.

" Thro' the world a spectral Shepherd
Walk'd, knee-deep in blood of martyrs,—
Death the Christ, whom men call'd Jesus,
Till they crown'd him Pope, at Rome !

XX.

"Meantime, I, the Accurst, was busy!
I who firstly to the Titan
Brought the fire of human knowledge,
Love for man and scorn for godhead.

"While the poets, priests, and prophets,
Libel'd me beyond believing,
Pictured me a shameless Devil
Cloven-footed and obscene,

"I was strengthening my children !
I was comforting and cheering
Many a martyr in his prison,
Pale and ready for the stake!

"Nay, my word had raised Mohammed,
Strong and true, a creed-compeller,
Spite the foolish Christian leaven
Mingled with his nobler clay.

" From the East I brought the Arabs
With their wondrous arts of healing ;
Small yet strong and cabalistic
Rose my mystic Alphabet !

" Out of fire I snatch'd the parchments
Scribbled o'er with ancient wisdom,
Pluck'd the books of Aristotle
From the cess-pools of the Pope.

" While the countless priests were lying,
I was preaching and beseeching—
Crying ' The eternal godhead
Helps but those who help themselves;

' " Pestilence, Disease, and Famine
Phantoms are of God's creation—
Man alone hath power to slay them,
Knowing good and knowing evil ;

" ' Eat, then, of the Tree of knowledge,
As your parents did in Eden—
Eat, and though your limbs be naked
Earth will yield you decent clothing !

H

" ' God who knoweth, feeleth nothing,
Cannot help you !—Tho' 'tis written
Not a sparrow falls without Him,
Ne'ertheless—the sparrow falls !'

" Yea, by Hades, I was busy !
In the monasteries even,
Many a learnéd monk was lesson'd
By the Devil whom he dreaded ;

" While the shaven head was nodding
Over parchment and papyrus,
I persuaded the good fellow
To transcribe my carnal books !

" Aye, and in their written Bibles,
Full of priestly contradictions,
I contrived to mingle deftly
Human truths with holy lies.

" True it is, indeed, I tempted
Both St. Anthony and Luther—
Proving to their consternation
Only fools despise the Flesh !

" I it was who fired the Painters,
Bade them fling upon the canvas
Holy Infants and Madonnas
Warm with nakedness and love ;

" I it was who made them picture
Christ the Shepherd, sweet and human,
Bright and young, with fond eyes gazing
On the rosy Magdalena !

" Thus with Life and Love and Beauty
War'd I on the side of Nature,
Knowing well that Man's salvation
Must be wrought of flesh and blood !

" Yea, and to the Priest I whisper'd :
' Rise erect, thou Beast, in manhood !
Reverence thy sex and function—
Snatch the fruits of Love and Joy !

" ' He who scorns the Flesh despises
Nature's Holiest of Holies—
In the Body's Temple only
Burns that mystic lamp, the Soul ! '

" I alone, whom men call'd Devil,
I, who fought for Truth and Knowledge,
I, the scorn'd and fabled Serpent,
Loved the human form divine !

" ' Crouch no more to gods or idols,
Crawl no more in filth and folly,
Stand erect,' I cried to mortals,
' Take your birthright, and be free!

" ' What ye take not freely, boldly,
From the brimming hands of Nature,
God the Lord will never give you,—
God the Lord gives all, yet nothing ! '

" Still they heark'd to their bell-wether !
Still they stumbled in the shambles,
Still they fumbled with their crosses,
Dwindling back to brutes and beasts.

" Westward then I sent Columbus !
Southward then I sent Magellan !
Starward, sunward, I, the Devil,
Turn'd Galileo's starry eyes !

" Crying, while the screech-owl Churches
Shriek'd their twenty-fold damnations,
' See and know ! demand your birthright !
Search the suns and map the spheres ! ' "

XXI.

For a space the starry splendour
Flash'd upon him out of Heaven,
As, with eager arms extended,
Angel-like he upward gazed;

Then again the cloud of sorrow
Fell upon him; darkly drooping,
Grew his form more sadly human,
As he proudly spoke again.

" While the tribes of priests and liars
Rear'd their shrines and lazar-houses,
Sold their charms and absolutions,
Did their clumsy Miracles,

" I, to shame their winking Virgins,
Sweating Christs, and minor marvels,
Was with all my might preparing
For a Miracle indeed !

" Of my letters cabalistic
Tiny blocks of wood I fashion'd,
Ranged them patiently in order,
(Chuckling slyly up my sleeve);

" Then I fasten'd them together,
Smear'd them o'er with ink from Hades,
Stamp'd the words on leaves papyric,—
And the Miracle was done !

" I, the Devil, invented Printing !
Calling to my aid the youngest
Of my sons, my little darling
Benjamin, the Printer's Devil.

" First I printed (mark my cunning !)
God's own Book, the Christian Bible,
Turn'd it out in fine black letter,
So that he who ran might read !

" Thus, observe, I pin'd the churchmen
Down to very verse and chapter !
Thus, Sir, for the good times coming,
I was nailing Lie on Lie !

" This was only the beginning
Of my Miracle ! The moment
I produced that great invention,
Light and Liberty were born !

" Suddenly arose and blossom'd
Man's new Tree of Good and Evil,
Shedding forth its leaves abundant,
Ripening to golden fruit !

" Large it grew and ever larger,
Ever putting forth fresh members,—
' Lop it ! cut it down ! destroy it ! '
Cried the churchmen, shriek'd the Popes.

" All the priests of all the Churches
Rush'd to smite it with their axes,—
Fools ! for every twig so smitten
Out there sprang a magic branch !

" As from some strong oak, moreover,
Growing in the merry greenwood,
From my Tree of Good and Evil
Acorns dropt, and oaklings sprouted ;

" Little birds pick'd up the acorns,
Dropt them down in distant places,—
Wheresoe'er the seed was carried,
New trees rose, till forests grew !

" ' Shun that leafage diabolic !
' Ware that wicked fruit of Knowledge ! '
Croak'd the ravens of the Churches,
Hovering o'er it in the air ;

" But the maiden and the lover
Sat beneath its shade and listen'd,
While the merry leaves were lisping
Songs that shepherds sang of yore ;

" Here the foot-sore and the weary,
Creeping from the dusty highway,
Lay beneath and hearken'd smiling
To the magic talking branches ;

" Kings arrived with trains attendant
Saying ' Here at least 'tis pleasant ! '
From my magic Tree they gather'd
Runes of Norseland, Tales of Troy.

"Reaching to my Tree, Erasmus
Gather'd gentle leaves of learning,
On the greensward underneath it
Petrarch and his Laura walk'd!

"Even rough old Martin Luther
Pluck'd a leaf and smiled approval!
Gazing upward in the starlight,
Abelard wept, and Tasso sang!

"Nay, the very monks came flocking
Open-mouth'd to look and listen,—
Charm'd they slyly sow'd my seedlings
In the monastery garden!

"Wheresoe'er my Tree enchanted
Spread its branches cabalistic,
Gladness grew, and wise men gather'd,
And 'twas Fairyland once more!

"Vain were all their winking Virgins,
Sweating Christs, and minor marvels,—
I, the Devil, had done the latest,
Greatest Miracle of all!

XXII.

" Since that hour the Fight hath lasted !
Strong, beneficent, and gentle,
I, the foe of all the Churches,
Have remain'd the friend of Man.

" All the horde of Priests and Prophets,
Moonstruck, mad, have rail'd against me,
Crying to the weary nations
' Fear the Flesh, and shun the Devil ! '

" In the name of God the Father
They have sicken'd Earth with slaughter ;
In the name of their Messiahs
They have lied, and lied, and lied !

" O'er the vineyards I have planted
They have scatter'd seed of thistles ;
In the mansions of my making
They have swarm'd with fire and sword.

" Year by year, with God against me,
I for Humankind have striven,
Winning patiently and slowly
Thro' a small minority !

" Poor are all the Church's martyrs,
By the side of mine, the Devil's !
Those have died for Filth and Falsehood,
These for Liberty and Light !

" Mine the Seers and mine the Poets,
Stoned and slain in every nation !
Even those who most denied me
Learn'd thro' *me* to stand erect !

" I it was who put the honey
On the tongue of Ariosto !
I who cast a light from Heaven
On Boccacio's golden page !

" In the ear of many a monarch
I was whispering my reasons—
Taught by me, your bluff King Harry
Faced the Pope and flay'd the cowls !

" Aye, and in your throned Virgin
I inspired both wit and learning—
I was hunting gladly with her,
When she whipt the wolves of Spain.

" While the Priests were busy burning,
I created Merrymakers !
Rock'd, despite the shrieking Churches,
Rabelais in his easy-chair !

" In your land of fogs and vapours,
Where the church-bells toll'd for ever,
I, the Devil, upraised the DRAMA
Still by priestcraft shun'd and curst :

"First I bribed the monks to help me,
Made them place on mimic stages
(Little 'ware. what they were doing)
Plays of miracles absurd.

" God Himself and little Jesus
Were by mortals represented,
While myself and other devils
Join'd them in the pagan dance.

"Thus, without a word of warning,
Rose the THEATRE, *my* Temple!
Sunny as the soul of Nature,
Fearless, beautiful, and free!

"'Shun it! shun the Devil's dwelling!'
Shriek'd the jealous cowls; but straightway,
Loud, the prelude of the battle,
Thunder'd Marlowe's mighty line!

"There I taught your gentle Shakespere
What no shaven monk could teach him—
Mingled wit and wisdom, foreign
To a God who never smiles!

"Churchmen curst, and still are cursing
What transcends their sermonizing,
Hating, in the way of traders,
Rival shops with smarter wares.

"In my Temple rose the voices
Of the Seers and Music-makers,—
Shapes of beauty and of terror
Waken'd to the conjuration!

" There the glad green world was pictured,
There the lark sang ' tirra-lirra,'
There the piteous human pageant
Broke to tears or rippled laughter—

" ' Shun it, shun the Devil's dwelling ! '
Croaked the jackdaws from the steeple—
Long as Shakespere's lark is singing,
Still my Theatre shall stand ! . . . .

" Then I mock'd their tracts and sermons
With my songs and my romances :
Light and Freedom, Mirth and Music,
Scatter'd sunshine through the air.

" Milton even, tho' intending
To exalt the Lord Almighty,
Spread my teaching Manichœan—
Who's his hero ?—I, the Devil !

" Aye, and when his voice demanded
Freedom for my printing presses,
Liberty of speech for all men,
Who inspired him ?   I, the Devil !

" Then, to mock their monkish fables,
I invoked *my* Story-tellers !
Till at last, full-blown and bounteous,
Bloom'd the Modern Novelist !

" True, the Novel is elephantine,
Pachydermatous, long-winded,
Of all Art the large negation,
Yet, by Heaven ! it serves a turn !

" My Cervantes and my Fielding
Struck the rock of human knowledge,
Freed the founts of Fun, still foreign
To a God who never laughs !

" How the Priests and Preachers trembled
At my quips and cranks and fancies,
Furious when I requisition'd
Rogues, like Sterne, within the fold !

" Evermore my printing presses
Labour'd, and across my kingdom,
Thick as leaves in Vallombrosa,
Fell the merry carnal books !

" Then, like sunshine made incarnate,
Rose the merry Djinn of Fiction,—
How the laughter of my Dickens
Scared the ravens and the owls !

" Then, the knell of all ascetics
Sounded, as my Reade upstarted,
Flooding all the gloomy Cloister
With the fires of Hearth and Home !

XXIII.

" Meantime, God had not been idle !
Angry at my benefactions,
He was wakening very slowly
To the peril long impending. . . .

" Over yonder, where the people
Groan'd like oxen yoked together,
Goaded on o'er stony fallows
By the Princes and the Priests,

" Where the Abbé curl'd and scented
Told his beads and lay with harlots,
While the Christ of Superstition
Dallied with the Pompadour,

" I, the Devil, in indignation
Raised my periwig'd *Alter Ego,*
Darling son of my adoption,
Whom the people named Voltaire !

" Diabolically smiling,
Up to Priest and Prince he strutted,
Tap'd his snuff-box, and politely
Crack'd his jokes at the Madonna!

" Nought of holy reputation
Scaped the ribald rascal's laughter—
Far away as Rome the Churches
Echo'd with his jests profane.

" Then behold, a transformation!
Suddenly he rose transfigured,
Periwig and snuff-box vanish'd,
And an Angel stood reveal'd!

" In his hand my sword of Freedom
Flashing on the eyes of Europe,—
While the hounds of persecution
Paused, and Calas kiss'd his feet!

" Then, while far as Rome the tumult
Rang, and voices shriek'd ' destroy him!'
' Lo 'tis Antichrist arisen!
Smite him, in the name of God!'

" At the lifting of my finger
Stormy spirits gather'd round him—
Strong and calm arose Condorcet,
Strong and fierce stood Diderot.

" Day by day the war was waging,—
I, the Devil, and my Titans,
'Gainst the God of Popes and Bibles
And his deputies on earth !

" Till at last the flames of battle
Caught the curtains of the palace,—
Panic stricken 'mong the people
Rush'd a monarch God-anointed.

" Then began the conflagration,—
Mitres, crosiers, crowns and sceptres,
Mingled up with moaning mortals,
Fed the ever increasing fires !

" I, the Devil, wept for pity,
While the bale-fires rose to Heaven,—
I, the Ishmael of the Angels,
Sicken'd at the fumes of blood.

" Midst that carnage all the cruel
Parasites of God were busy,—
IGNORANCE, his page-in-waiting,
DEATH, his master of the hounds!

" Vainly to the madden'd people
Cried my Titans, interceding
For the innocent and gentle
Seized to feed the conflagration.

" Not a hair of beast and mortal
Ever fell through *me*, the Devil,—
From the first my rebel spirit
Bled and wept for the afflicted.

"Death and Pain were God's conception,
Never mine, the Prince of Pity's!
If they dwell within my kingdom,
I, the Devil, am not to blame.

" I for ages after ages
Had proclaimed the truth to mortals—
' God is powerless to redeem you,
In yourselves abides salvation ;

" ' Love each other, help each other,
Eat the golden fruit forbidden,—
Out of Knowledge ripely gather'd
Wisdom comes and Freedom grows !' . . .

" Out of evil, evil springeth,—
Even so, in Hell and Paris,   ·
Centuries of evil sowing
Turn to aftermath of Hate !

" Lastly, from the conflagration
Sprang a spirit, man or Devil,—
Whether God or I begat him
I could never quite discover !

" Diabolically clever,
Strong as any of my Titans,
Impudent as any Devil,
Rose the little Corporal ! . . .

" I incline to think the fellow
Was a sort of blood-relation
Who, by lust of loot perverted,
Join'd the legions of the Lord !

" O'er the nations sick with slaughter
Many a night and day he gallopt—
God had lent him Death's White Charger
(Well described in *Revelations*) ;

" Death himself, afoot, ran after
With the hosts of the Grand Army,
Feeding well, where'er he followed,
On the flesh and blood of mortals. . . .

" After all, and on reflection,
I reject this Demi-devil,
Since within his soul there quicken'd
Neither love nor human kindness,

" (Which, I hold, are the supremest
Qualities of true revolters) ;—
Yes, God played a trick upon me,
Thro' a devilish renegade !

" Down in Hell are decent people,
Honest souls who love their fellows ;—
To the cruel God of Battles
I relinquish Buonaparté ! "

XXIV.

All the glory of the Angel
Now had utterly departed—
Quietly he now addressed me,
Calm and modern as at first ;

.

On the lonely Heath at Hampstead
Sat my Devil, grimly smiling,
In his hand the evening journal,
Spectacles upon his nose. . . .

" Troubled by the devastation
Laying waste my little kingdom,
Showing that the Lord Almighty
Wrought against me as of old ;

" Sick because the blinded masses
Clamour'd still for signs and portents,
' Time it surely is,' I mutter'd,
' For another Miracle ! '

" So, my Benjamin assisting,
I the NEWSPAPER invented—
'Gainst the Church's red batallions
Rose at last the thin black line !

" Nought that Priests and Tyrants plotted,
Nought that mortals did or suffer'd,
Nought that passes on this planet,
Any more remained in darkness !

" Nay, I tamed the very Lightning
To assist my revelations—
Thro' the night it took its tidings
Flashing into fiery words !

" On the walls of hut and palace
Flamed my messages to mortals—
Startled 'mid the feast, Earth's rulers
Looked aghast at one another !

" All the affairs of Hell and Heaven
By my servants were recorded,—
I had watchful correspondents
Even in the Vatican !

" For the first time human creatures
Knew, the affliction of their fellows—
Tyrants blush'd to find recorded
Deeds they had not blush'd to do !

" O my Benjamin, the youngest
Of my sons, the Printer's Devil !
I myself at times was startled
At the rogue's irreverence !

" Nought that God had done in darkness
Could escape his circumspection !
All the evils God created
Now were patent to the world ! "

" Even so," I answer'd quickly,
" Thanks to thee, O woeful Spirit,   .
Ever prying and denying,
Nought is hid from eyes profane ;

" Ignorance is at last completed
By this thing of thy creation,—
Foul as any other priestcraft
Is the priestcraft of the Press !

" Clamour of thy Printer's Devil
Silences the wise and holy,
Life grows hideous, while his shameful,
Shameless scandals fill the air ;

" By the filth thou namest Knowledge
All the springs of life are poison'd,—
Foul St. Simeons of the column
Pose, and proffer absolution !

" Poison of thy fiends was scatter'd
On the world-worn eyes of Coleridge ;
Poison'd daggers of thy devils
Stab'd to Keats's heart of hearts !

" Foulest of all human follies
Is the Newspaper !" I added—
" Art and all things fair and holy
Fade at last before its breath !"

Scornfully he smiled upon me,—
" Grant," he said, " my servant blunders ;
In a scheme so democratic
Individual merit fails.

" Yet, with all its limitations,
This, the latest of my labours,
Is a boon of light and leading
To the woe-worn race of men.

" Priests have cried, ' Let there be darkness !
Hide away the truths thou fearest !'
I, the Devil, being wiser,
Cry, ' Let Truth and Light prevail !'

" By the printed words, the record
Of the conscience of the people,
By my clamouring Printer's Devil,
Freedom spreads from land to land :

" Deeds of night no more are hidden,
Deeds of grace are multiplying ;
Light into the dungeon flowing
Strikes the fetters of the slave.

" At my printed protestation
On his throne the Tyrant trembles :
Words of hope, for Freedom utter'd,
Shake the footstool of the Czar !

" Even the lying leader writer
Pillories the God he praises !
Even the critic speeds the triumph
Of the Seer he mocks and scorns !

" Ever in my open daylight
Truth and Falsehood stand together—
In the daylight Falsehood withers,
Truth is known and justified !

" Those who serve your God Almighty
Cry aloud ' The Light is hateful ! '
In the night His Church has flourish'd,
In the daylight it doth fall !

" War not, in thy soul's impatience,
'Gainst my busy benediction !
Rail not, Poet, 'gainst my Devils,
Wroth because they will not praise thee !

" If thy soul be just and gentle,
Be thou sure that men shall know it !
If thy song be great and deathless,
God nor Devil can destroy it !

" I, the Devil, refuse to foster
Vanity in God or poets !
Both believe in loaves and fishes
And in fulsome adulation.

" I, the Devil, am democratic !
For the general good I labour—
Those who would be prais'd and petted
I relinquish to the Tories.

"Tennyson I liked extremely
(Even pardon'd him for praising
That white sepulchre, King Arthur)
Till he join'd the House of Lords.

Light and Knowledge for the masses,
Speech for Wisdom and for Folly,
These I claim, and even the zany
May announce his zanyhood ;

" Busily my printing presses
Publish all things, good or evil ;
When my Printer's Devil blunders
Tis at least in open day.

"Light is Death to Falsehood ever!
Light illumes my printing presses!
Ev'n thro' fools my truth shall triumph
And my Demos witch 'the world!"

XXV.

For a space he paused, and gazing
Proudly upward to the heavens,
Where the countless constellations
Clustered close as if to listen,

Lost he seem'd in contemplation
Of the shining lights above him,
While the soft celestial splendour
On his woe-worn face was raining.

"Heir," he said, " of all Earth's sorrow,
Brother of those lonely spirits
Who on yonder stars and planets
Still perform their tasks allotted,

"I, the outcast Prince of Pity,
Have at last to Man unfolded
All the story of Creation,
Birth and Death, and Evolution.

" I have taught him how to measure
Yonder spheres and their processions,—
Seizing for his apprehension
God's abstractions, Space and Time!

" What Galileo dreamed, what Bruno
Guess'd from sleepless inspiration,
I at last have demonstrated
Thro' the mouths of mighty thinkers.

" Open lies the Book of Heaven!
Children even may read its pages,—
Stranger far than any fable
Is the record of Creation!

" Nay, the mind of Man may follow
God into the depths of darkness—
From the wonders Seen divining
Those Unseen, and yet not hidden!

" By my symbols algebraic
I have counted lands and waters,
With my chemics cabalistic
I have solved the Elemental!

K

"Further, to the sight of mortals,
I the womb of Earth have open'd—
Showing how, through endless ages,
Man's strange embryos were fashion'd !

"Nay, and to their wondering vision
I have map'd the life within them—
Clear as yonder starry Heaven
Lies the microcosm, Man !

"Wondrous as the Light lifegiving
Thro' the Universe pulsating,
Floweth Light in Man, the Unit,
From the heart, its central Sun.

"As the cell that builds the planet
Is the cell that builds the mortal—
As the greater is the lesser,
As the lesser is the greater.

"Thro' my love and benediction
Man has plumb'd the abyss of Being—
By the law that never endeth
Life and Death revolve for ever.

"ALL THE ARTS BY GOD FORBIDDEN,
ALL THE KNOWLEDGE HID IN DARKNESS,
I REVEAL!"

" All the arts by God forbidden,
All the knowledge hid in darkness,
I reveal, while the Creator
Rests in impotence of Godhead.

" Nay, I show that God is fetter'd
· By the chains of His own making—
Blind and bound He broods, while Nature
Moveth on in calm progression.

" Thro' my love and benediction
Man hath learn'd the gifts of Healing—
Now for every Church that falleth
Hospitals arise to Heaven ;

" Strong, beneficent, and gentle,
Christs of surgery and leechcraft
Work their wonders, far more holy
Than the marvels of Messiahs.

" Wheresoever Death is busy
Fly my ministers of blessing,
Snatching ever from his talons
Creatures beautiful and fair.

" Cast thy look along the Ages !
Read the record of the Churches !
Pestilence, Disease, and Famine
Fill the footprints of the Christ !

" Thro' the very Fruit Forbidden,
Thro' the laws of Light and Knowledge,
I have fought with Death and Evil,
Conquering, in despite of God—

" Curst, and yet the source of blessing,
Outcast, yet supreme 'mong Angels,
I, the only true Redeemer,
Work my miracles for men ! "

XXVI.

Smiling scornfully, I answer'd :—
" Strange it seems to find the Devil,
Spite a record so despairing,
Optimistic, after all !

" Yet, methinks, thy boasted Demos
Is the very worst of tyrants !
Better far a single Cæsar
Than a Cæsar hydra-headed !

" Gaze again upon thy kingdom !
Look on Rome !   As *thou* didst wander
In the streets of Rome departed,
Sick of God and God's creation,

" So from day to day I wander
In the City of thy Demos,—
Demos is a fouler Cæsar,
London is a lewder Rome !

" Still the Priests and Seers and Prophets
Preach the faith they feel no longer—
Keeping to the ear the promise
They have broken to the Soul;

" Still the slaves and tyrants palter
With the truth they dare not utter—
Still the spectral Man of Sorrows
Starveth at the Church's door;

" Still, to blind the foolish people,
With the worn-out creed men juggle,—
Even o'er their cheating parchments
Smiling lawyers hold the Cross;

" Atheist judges, cold and cruel,
Toss the murtherer to the hangman,
Crying, while they shrug their shoulders,
' God have mercy on thy soul! '

" Dark and dissolute and dreadful
As that other Rome departed,
Is this later Rome and lewder,—
Death is crownéd *here* as *there* !

" Last, thy Demos, while denying
All Divinity, assevers
He's essentially a Christian,
Since he leads a moral life ! "

Smiling quietly my Devil
Answer'd, " True, O angry Poet—
There my Demos errs : Messiahs
Always are immoral persons !

" If the Christ of Superstition
Work'd no miracles or wonders,
If the man was well-conducted,
He was surely no Messiah ! "

Sadly, wearily, he added :
" Here as in the Rome departed
Priests abide and Folly lingers,
Conquering in the name of God ;

" Priests abide, but Death is reigning !
Thus, in spite of God, I triumph !
Patience, patience, for my Demos
Groweth wiser day by day !

" 'Tis the way of foolish mortals,
When they cease to feel religion,
To become severely moral,
Hating Liberty and Light—

" So, I grant, my woe-worn Demos
Makes Morality his fetish,
Closing ears and shutting eyelids
To the sanctions of the Flesh.

" Patience, patience ! I will teach him
Love that passeth understanding !
All the wondrous lore of Nature
Shall be open to his gaze !

" This, at least, is certain :   Never
Will he lose again his birthright !
Never bend before his tyrants,
Here on earth, or there in Heaven !

" Never will he kneel and listen
To the lies of your Messiahs,
Forfeit for a fancied blessing
Light and Liberty and Life !

" Patience, patience ! Light is growing—
God at last shall be forgotten—
Man shall rise erect, subduing
All things evil, even Death ! "

XXVII.

" If thou speakest truth," I answer'd,
" Much, indeed, thou hast been libel'd !
Yet thy very benedictions
Spring from Him, the first Creator.

" By the will of Him, the Father,
Thou hast wrought to cleanse thy kingdom—
From the first His eyes, all-seeing,
Knew thee as His instrument !

" If Mankind, tho' dimly, darkly,
Moveth onward to perfection,
If at last the ills of Nature
Shall be heal'd and render'd whole,

" Even there I trace the Finger
Of the Almighty slowly working,
Till the hour when *thou*, His servant,
Kneeling low, shalt be forgiven !

" Then Humanity, made holy,
Kneeling also to the Father,
Shall accept His final blessing
And be lifted up and saved ! "

Wistfully he lookt upon me,
Once again his face was clouded
With that mist of woeful pity,
While his eyes grew dim with tears. , , .

Then, another transformation !
Bright and radiant, tho' despairing,
Rose he to his angel's stature,
Looking up with starry orbs ;

While the stars and constellations
Fixing countless eyes upon him,
Shed upon his woe-worn features
Splendour from a million worlds,

In a voice like stars vibrating,
Answer'd by the hosts of Heaven,
Cried he, while his troubled spirit
Shook with woeful indignation :

" Cast thy thought along the Ages !
Walk the sepulchres of Nations !
Mourn, with *me*, the fair things perish'd !
Mark the martyrdoms of men !

" Say, can any latter blessing
Cleanse the blood-stain'd Book of Being ?
Can a remnant render'd happy
Wipe out centuries of sorrow ?

" Nay, one broken life outweigheth
Twenty thousand lives made perfect !
Nay, I scorn the God whose pathway
Lieth over bleeding hearts !

" From the first the cry of anguish
Hath arisen to yonder Heaven !
From the first, the ways of Nature
Have been cruel and accurst !

" Man, thou say'st, shall *yet* be happy ?
What avails a bliss created
Out of hetacombs of evil,
Out of endless years of pain ?

"Happy? Looking ever backward
On the graves of generations,
Haunted by the eyes despairing
Of the millions lost for ever ?

" Even now the life he liveth
Builded is of shame and sorrow !
Even now his flesh is fashion'd
Of the creatures that surround him !

" From the sward the stench of slaughter
Riseth hourly to his nostrils !
By his will the beast doth anguish
And the wounded dove doth die !

" Dreamer ! Even here thy fancy
Fails before the truths of Nature—
God, thy great all-loving Father,
By His will created Death !—

"Like the races long departed,
So the perfect race shall perish !
Like the suns burnt out and faded,
Shall thy sun be shrivell'd up !

" Juggle not with words and phrases !
Lie not with the Priests and Prophets !
Pain and Death are God's creation,
And eternal, like Himself !

" I alone, whom men call Devil,
Have allay'd the woes of Nature !
Death alone I cannot vanquish—
Death and God, perchance, are One !"

XXVIII.

Oh, the sorrow and the splendour
Of that woe-worn Outcast Angel!
Reverently I bent before him,
Blessing him, the Prince of Pity;

Round him, as he look'd to Heaven,
Clung a cloud of golden music—
Fair he seem'd as when, ere fallen,
Singing on the morning star!

"Thus," he said, "throughout the ages,
O'er the world my feet have wander'd,
Watching in eternal pity
Endless harvest-fields of Death!

"One by one the tribes and races
To the silent grave have waver'd,—
Never have I seen a sleeper
Slip his shroud, to rise again!

" Dead they lie, the strong, the gentle,
Dead alike, the good and evil,—
Dust to dust, ashes to ashes,
All is o'er—they rest at last !

.

" All the tears of all the martyrs
Fall'n in vain for Man's redemption !
All the souls of all the singers
Dumb for ever in the grave !

" Where are they whose busy fingers
Wove the silks of Tyre and Sidon ?
Where are they who in the desert
Raised the mighty Pyramids ?

" Ants upon an ant-heap, insects
Of the crumbling cells of coral,
Coming ever, ever going,
Race on race has lived and died.

" Ev'n as Babylon departed,
So shall yonder greater City ;
Like the Assyrian, like the Roman,
Celt and Briton shall depart !

" Yea, the Cities and the Peoples
One by one have come and vanish'd :
Broken, on the sandy desert,
Lies the Bull of Nineveh !

" Ev'n as beauteous reefs of coral
Rising bright and many-colour'd
In the midst of the great waters,
Wondrous Nations have arisen ;

" First the insects that upbuilt them
Labour'd busily, and dying
Left the reef of their creation
Crumbling wearily away ;

" O'er the reef the salt ooze gathers,
Mud and sand are heapt upon it,
Then the trees and flowers and grasses
Bury it for evermore !

" Shall I bend in adoration
To the Lord of these delusions ?
Nay, I stand erect, and scorn Him,—
Pulseless, null Omnipotence !

L

" Deaf to all the wails and weeping,

Blind to all the woes of Being,

Plunging daily into darkness

All the dreams of all the Christs ! "

XXVIII.

"Nay," I cried, "the Christ shall triumph!
After centuries of sorrow
Man at last shall gain his birthright
And arise, a living Soul!

"Proves not this that One above thee
Wrought in love from the beginning?
Creeds and systems come and vanish,
But the Law Divine abides!

"Out of endless tribulation
Springs the Human, casting from him
One by one the sins and sorrows
Worn in ignorance of godhead;

"All around him and within him
Lies His kingdom, but He rules it
By the grace of One Supremer
Who created it and *him*!

" ' Know thyself ! ' the Voice Eternal
Crieth ; and himself he knoweth,
God incarnate, bowing meekly
To the Eternal Voice and Law.

" Even thus thy God hath conquer'd !
What thy spirit wrought against Him
Turneth ever to a witness
Of His glory everlasting !

" Kneel, then, rebel, and adore Him !
Kneel with Man and chant His praises,
Hallelujah to the Highest,
As 'twas sung in the beginning ! "

Pallid in the moonlight, turning
Sad eyes upward to the Heavens,
Head erect, still proud in sorrow,
Stood that weary fallen Spirit !

" Fool," he answer'd, " what availeth ?
Praise or prayer or lamentation ?
Blindly, pitilessly, surely,
Worketh the Eternal Law.

" Dust to dust, ashes to ashes !
Nought escapeth, nought abideth—
Man, the sand for ever shifting
In an hour-glass, cometh, goeth !

" Death alone is King and Master !
Death is mightiest here and yonder,—
Man, the drop within a fountain,
Riseth ever, ever falleth !

" Vain the Dream and the Endeavour !
Vain the quest of Love and Knowledge,—
Man, the dewdrop in the Rainbow,
Shineth, then is drunk for ever !

" Answerest thou, that *nought* can perish ?
That the elements for ever
Disappearing, re-emerging,
Shape themselves to Life anew ?

" Even so ; but Death shall silence
All that forms thy human nature—
Memory, consciousness, self-knowledge,
Personality, and Love !

" Out of darkness God hath drawn thee,
Back to darkness thou returnest—
In that moment of thy making
Thou becam'st a conscious Soul!

" Loving, hoping, apprehending,
Yearning to the Souls around thee,—
Father, mother, wife and children,
Sharers of thy joy and sorrow;

" These are *thou*, and these must vanish
Leaving not a trace behind them—
With the Elemental godhead
Thou and these shall mix for ever!

" The Supreme, the Elemental,
Voiceless is, and all unconscious!
But the conscious type emerging
Shineth, and is trumpet-tongued!

" From the dark he cometh, standing
Beautiful and demigod-like,
Crying gladly, ' Lo my kingdom,
Where I reign as God's anointed ' ;

" Knowing, feeling, apprehending,
Thus he cometh to his birthright—
Memory, consciousness, self-knowledge,
Personality, and Love !

" Fool, Death taps him on the shoulder,
Death, the wraith of the Almighty,
Saying, ' Cease !   The law of being
Meaneth endless retrogression !

" ' Back into the Night ! re-mingle
With the elemental Darkness !
Only for a little moment
God permits thee to abide ! '

" Broken-hearted and despairing,
Into silence he returneth—
Dust to dust, ashes to ashes !
Crush'd he lies, a crumbling shell !

" Name me not the Prince of Evil,—
Call me still the Prince of Pity,
Since alone among immortals
I have wept for human woes !

"What remaineth?   One thing only,
Since Death cometh soon or later :
Carpe diem !   While it lasteth,
Stand erect, Ephemeron !

" Waste no thought on the Almighty ;
Seek, with all thy soul's endeavour,
How to make thine earthly dwelling
Bright and fair, in God's despite !

" Only for a day thou livest !
Make that day, so quickly fleeting,
For thyself, for all thou lovest,
Beautiful with Light and Joy !

" Yet, the pity ! ah, the pity !
Back, far back, along the ages,
Stretch the graves of countless creatures
Who have borne the Cross for *thee* !

" *They*, too, loved the light that lieth
On the seas and on the mountains !
They, too, by their God forsaken,
Died at last on Calvary !

" *They*, too, dreamed of Life Eternal !
They, too, knelt before the Father !
They, too, clung to one another,
Till He drave them back to dust ! "

XXIX.

As he spake, I saw around me
Once again the Apparitions
Moving ant-wise hither and thither
'Neath the glimpses of the moon;

Faces of the dead departed
Glimmer'd on me from the shadows,
While a sound of woeful voices
Faintly wailing fill'd the air;

And again (which still was strangest!)
Never one did gaze upon me,
Though I named them, wildly sobbing,
Stretching hungry empty arms;

Then at last my soul within me
Sicken'd, and the air around me,
Ev'n as seas around the drowning,
Swung,—till sense and sight departed! . . .

XXX.

On the lonely Heath of Hampstead
I awoke, and as I waken'd
Saw the Devil departing from me
Thro' the shadows of the night;

Limping lame, and bending double,
Like a venerable mortal,
Round he turn'd, before he vanish'd,
Sigh'd, and fixed his eyes on mine.

(Ah, the sleepless eyes, so woeful
With the wisdom of the Serpent!
Ah, the piteous face, so weary
With the woes of all the worlds!)

Forcing then his wrinkled features
To a smile, and grimly laughing—
" Plead," he said, " for the Defendant !
Be my Laureate, yet remember :

" If the priests were right, and yonder
Waited Heaven and compensation,
I'd at once admit my folly,
Taking off my hat to God !"

Nodding quietly, he vanish'd,
While again I sadly wander'd
O'er the lonely Heath of Hampstead,
Thro' the silence of the Night. . . .

XXXI.

Little did I dream or fancy
I should ever (God forgive me !)
State the Case for the Defendant
Whom I loath'd with all my soul !

From a race of cattle stealers,
Rievers of the clan Buchanan,
I, Buchanan, sprang—the riever's
Savage blood is in my veins ;

Thieves and wolves we were, but never
Foxes, and our Celtic motto
Reads in Roman lingo—" *Magnest
Veritas, et prevalebit* ! "

Tell the truth and shame the Devil !
Tell it, even tho' it praise him !
Tell the truth for the Defendant,
Tho' the Accuser be thy God !

Better still—let the Defendant
Plead his Case in his own person:
Tho' it means thine own damnation
Let the awful truth prevail ! . . . : . . . .

Yet, alas ! that happy Eden !
All the golden, gladsome Garden !
God the Father smiling on us,
Raining gentle blessings down !

Eve, that ne'er shalt be a mother,
Wrap thy sleeping shroud about thee !
All is over, all is over,—
But the Devil was *not* to blame !

FINIS.

EPILOGUE:

THE LITANY. DE PROFUNDIS.

THE LITANY. DE PROFUNDIS.

O God our Father in Heaven, Holy, Unseen, and
    Unknown,
Have mercy on us Thy children, who pray beneath Thy
    Throne!

O God our Father in Heaven, Holy, Unseen, and Unknown,
Have mercy on us Thy children, who pray beneath Thy Throne!

O God the Maker of Mortals, Life of all lives that be,
Speak, that our ears may hear Thee, shine, that our
    eyes may see!

O God the Maker of Mortals, Life of all lives that be,
Speak, that our ears may hear Thee, shine, that our eyes may see!

O God the Unbegotten, Fountain whence all things flow,
Open the rock of Thy Secret, that we may see Thee and
    know.

O God the Unbegotten, Fountain whence all things flow,
Open the Rock of Thy Secret, that we may see Thee and know.

Son that had never a Father, Father that never had Son,
Here on the Earth and yonder in Heaven, Thy will be
done.

Son that had never a Father, Father that never had Son,
Here on the Earth and yonder in Heaven, Thy will be done.

Remember not our offences, O Father and Lord Divine,
Pity and spare Thy children, whose sins and offences
are Thine;
For if they are blind and see not, 'tis Thou who closest
their eyes,
And if they are frail and foolish, 'tis Thou who shouldst
make them wise!
And be not angry, O Father, but sheathe Thine avenging
Sword,
Spare the things of Thy making, love them and spare
them, O Lord.

We are the things of thy making, spare us and love us, O
Lord.

From all things hateful and evil, which come O Father
from Thee,
From Sin, the Flesh, and the Devil, whom Thou per-
mittest to be,
From what through Thee we suffer, since Thou hast
made men thus,
From lesser and greater damnation, O Lord, deliver us!

From lesser and greater damnation, O Lord, deliver us!

From pride and from vain glory, from all hypocrisy,
From envy, hatred, and malice, and all uncharity,
From filth, from fornication, from all things vile and
abhorred
Which leaven the bread of Thy making, deliver us, O
Lord !

From filth, from fornication, from all things vile and abhorred
Which leaven the bread of Thy making, deliver us, O Lord !

From thine avenging Lightning ! from Fire and Famine
and Pest !
From all the terrors and portents Thy Will makes
manifest !
From War Thy witless Daughter, from Murder Thy
maniac Son,
From Death that at Thy bidding betrays us, Almighty
One,
From all Thy hand hath fashion'd to keep men mourning
thus,
From all the woes of Creation, good Lord, deliver us !

From all the woes of Creation, good Lord, deliver us !

We are the things of Thy making, we are the clouds of
Thy breath !
Life hast Thou made, O Father, to flee forever from
Death,
Flesh Thou hast wrapt around us, Flesh and the lusts of
the same,

Out of Thy Word 'twas fashion'd, out of Thy mouth
   they came !
From all the doubt and the darkness Thy vials of wrath
   have poured
To blind the spirits that seek Thee, deliver us, good
   Lord !

*From all the doubt and the darkness Thy vials of wrath have
   poured*
To blind the spirits that seek thee, deliver us, good Lord !

Thou hast set these Rulers above us, to bind us, to
   blind our eyes,
Thou hast sent these Priests to lure us with creeds and
   dogmas and lies,
Thou hast built Thy Church on the sands still shifting
   and tremulous,
From Churches, and Priests, and Liars, good Lord,
   deliver us !

From Churches, and Priests, and Liars, good Lord, deliver us !

By Thyself Incarnate within us, Thy Voice in our aching
   ears,
By Thy birth and Thy circumcision, Thy baptism of
   tears,
By fasting and by temptation, from all the passionate
   horde
Of Devils that seize and slay us, deliver us, good Lord.

By fasting and by temptation, from all the passionate horde
Of Devils that seize and slay us, deliver us, good Lord.

By the woe Thou hast never felt, by the Cross and the
    Crown of Thorn,
By the agony and the sweat on the brow of Thine Eldest
    Born,
By the cry that never was answer'd and ringeth ever
    aloud,
By the tomb that never was open'd, the dust therein,
    and the shroud,
By Him who sleepeth forever, while we implore Thee
    thus,
From Death and from tribulation, good Lord, deliver us !

From Death and from tribulation, good Lord, deliver us !

Strengthen our hearts to know Thee, O God that cannot
    be known !
Make righteous the Kings who rule us, and sit on an
    earthly throne !
Set in their hands Thy sceptre, place in their hands Thy
    sword—
Help us to bear their yoke !

    We beseech thee to hear us, good Lord !

Shine on the eyes of Thy Priests, illumine Thy Bishops,
    shed
Lightnings to quicken life in the creeds that are pulse-
    less and dead.
When the Holy supper is set, and the Ghost of the
    Christ at the board
Sits, be *Thou* there in our mid'st !

    We beseech thee to hear us, good Lord.

Instruct the Lords of the Council ! endow the brain of
the Fool !

Bless and preserve our Masters who sit in high places
and rule !

But when in their granaries yonder the harvest of toil
is stored,

Spare us some mouthfuls of bread !

We beseech Thee to hear us, good Lord.

Father that dwellest in Heaven, so far from the sorrows
of Earth,

Soften to us, Thy children, the travails of Death and of
Birth,

Teach us to love Thee and dread Thee, to eat the
bread of Thy Word,

Altho' it be hard as stone !

We beseech Thee to hear us, good Lord.

We beseech Thee to hear us, good Lord, when darkness
and sorrow are near us,

When blindly we grope thro' the dark, good Lord, we
beseech Thee to hear us,

We beseech Thee to hear us, good Lord, and send Thy
Spirit to cheer us !

*When Thy yoke is hardest to bear, good Lord, we beseech
Thee to hear us !*

Help us when we are falling, as we help others who
fall !

By land and by sea preserve us, O Father, Maker
    of all !

Comfort the sick and the weary with tidings of hope and
    of peace,

All children, all women who labour that what Thou
    hast made may increase,

Open the gates to the captive, lift up the weak and
    forlorn,

Feed, too, the fatherless orphans, comfort the widows
    that mourn.

Have mercy, Father in Heaven, and send Thy spirit to
    cheer us,

We beseech Thee to hear us, good Lord !

Good Lord, we beseech Thee to hear us !

O Father who canst not conquer our sorrow, since it is
    Thine !

Maker who cannot unmake us, since we, like Thee, are
    divine !

Light that dwellest within us, Light that art far away !

Nearest to, farthest from us, answer our prayers when
    we pray !

Lord, have mercy upon us ! Send thy Spirit to cheer
    us !

Have mercy and hear us, O Lord !

O Lord, have mercy and hear us !

Save us from all our enemies, Most High !

In our afflictions, Lord, be ever nigh !

Pity our sorrows, Fountain of all Light!
And when we pray be near us day and night!

Let us pray.

THE PRAYER.

Father, which art in Heaven, not here below!
   Be Thy Name hallowëd, in that place of worth!
And till Thy Kingdom cometh, and we know,
   Be Thy will done more tenderly on earth!
Since we must live, give us our daily bread!
   Forgive our stumblings, since Thou mad'st us blind!
If we offend Thee, Lord, at least forgive
   As tenderly as we forgive our kind.
Spare us temptation, human or divine!
   Deliver us from evil, now and then!
The Kingdom, Power, and Glory all are Thine
   For ever and for evermore.   Amen.

Let us pray.

O God, Unseen, Unknown, yet dimly guessed
   By spirit and by sense,
The miracle of Nature doth attest
   Thy dread Omnipotence!

Teach us to love Thee, God and Lord of all,
   And lead us to thy Light!
We love Thee not, we are too weak and small,
   And Thou too Infinite! . . . .

O God we have heard with our ears, and our fathers
   have told it unto us,
That Thou canst uplift or cast down, redeem, or forever undo us,
The works Thou hadst made we behold as dawn after
   dawn cometh breaking,
But evil and pain and despair are blent with the worlds
   of thy making,—
Unveil the light of Thy Face, till all Thy dread ways
   become clear to us !

Deliver us out of the Darkness ! Bend down thro' Thy clouds
   and give ear to us !

Glory be Thine, O Father, from all things fashion'd by
   Thee.

As it was in the beginning, is, and ever shall be !

*In the Press, and will be published immediately, New and
Cheaper Edition, with a new Preface and Notes.*

THE WANDERING JEW:

A Christmas Carol.

BY ROBERT BUCHANAN.

SOME PRESS AND PULPIT OPINIONS.

SPEAKER

What strikes us as most remarkable about Mr. Buchanan's poem,
and the remarkable discussion to which it has given rise, is the singular
parallelism between the whole matter and what is related in the New
Testament. Christ is being tried over again, at the instance of a furibund
Scotch poet, before a prætorium in Fleet Street.

SPECTATOR.

A stranger 'Christmas Carol' was never written. Mr. Buchanan's
poem may be described as a half-tremulous, half-wistful wail over the
gigantic failure of Christ. . This is, we say, the main drift of the
poem,—love for Christ, impatience with the Eternal Father for His delay
in securing Him His triumph. . . .

TIMES

Mr. Buchanan has essayed a task which would have taxed to the
uttermost the poetic genius of a Dante and a Milton combined. . . . For
the rest, Mr. Buchanan handles the rhymed couplet with no little variety
and skill, and he writes with powerful rhetoric.

ZEIT-GEIST (Berlin).

For many years no book has created such a tumult. . . . It is only
two weeks in the hands of the public, and already whole pages of the
newspapers are filled with what the poet says, and how he says it. . . .
Buchanan has produced a noteworthy and thought-inspiring book.

THE ROCK.

Honest and conscientious . . . but it is awful reading, and shocks us inexpressibly.

WORLD.

The leading idea of the poem is decidedly original, and the arraignment of Christ is magnificently dramatic. . . . It is not too much to say that the *Wandering Jew* should greatly improve the author's position as a writer and thinker.

ECHO.

Mr. Buchanan has given us a picture which he says will haunt us. The 'Wandering Jew' will fully justify the author's predictions. . . . Every line of the poem is reverent to the highest aspirations of man, and sympathetic to the woes of the central figure.

TELEGRAPH.

A strange, powerful, but also painful, piece of work. . . . Again and again instinct with imaginative force.

THE REV. HUGH PRICE HUGHES
(at the Conference in St. James's Hall).

Let me, then, say in the first place, that it will do all orthodox and devout Christians immense and endless good to read, ponder, and remember the attack upon historic and ecclesiastical Christianity which this poems utters. I say that nothing better could be done than that Robert Buchanan should rub these facts well into our ecclesiastical skins. I freely admit that through all the centuries the name of Christ has been identified with every kind of devilry. . . There is nothing in this terrible poem to give intelligent Christians fear.

THE REV. F. SLOPER.
(preaching in Congregational Church, Kilburn).

Strauss, Renan, and, we may add, Buchanan, will live in literature because they have attempted to do something with Jesus. Mr. Buchanan's poetry and philosophy show that it is Jesus, not Christianity, which is on trial.

BIRMINGHAM POST.

All this weltering mass of foul accusation is but the morbid dream of an egotistic rhymer.

MISS MARIE CORELLI (Author of " Barabbas ").

There would be something inexpressibly funny in a Robert Buchanan pronouncing doom on the Christ, if it were not so revolting.

THE REV. DR. CLIFFORD.
(*preaching in Westbourne Park Chapel*).

Mr. Buchanan's book is serviceable, in that, in the most eloquent and forcible terms, it has pointed out the way in which detrimental forces have been working. Yet, in spite of this, Christianity is Life.

MANCHESTER GUARDIAN.

Vigour, fervour, sweep, and a certain distinct touch of mystical passion which no one who remembers the ' Ballad of Judas Iscariot ' will deny.

LITERARY WORLD.

The most eloquent exposition of the school of religious pessimism which we have seen. The book exercises a fascination over the reader.

SUNDAY SUN.

Take the thing as a whole, and there is something even great about it. It is the conception of no mere literary pigmy. We should like to see the finicking minor poet who could bend this bow ! . . . Images of poetic beauty, pictures of weird fascination, narrative and descriptive passages of striking power. . . . He has done something which is likely to justify his own boast : ' In your dreams this thing will *haunt* you ! '

PARIS FIGARO.

The celebrated Scottish poet, Robert Buchanan, has just published a new poem, ' The Wandering Jew,' which is making a great stir in England. It is certainly Buchanan's *chef-d'œuvre*. Form and subject are alike remarkable, and the work deserves to be translated into all languages.

CHRISTIAN GLOBE.

The work is universally admitted to contain much powerful writing, and to be the fruit of an honest and even a reverent mind.

DR. JOSEPH PARKER.

I am not going to throw this brilliant genius into the waste paper basket. Mr. Buchanan is on his way to the true and eternal Altar.

THE REV. WILLIAM PIERCE.
(preaching at New Court Chapel.)

The wonderful picture portrayed by Mr. Buchanan.   . . All the same it is a highly blasphemous book. . . . [Mr. Pierce adds, in a letter to the ' Chronicle ' :] Its strength lies in the fact that contains a great deal that is true. There is no use denying it, the long story of mediæval Christianity is a monstrous repudiation of all that is truly Christian.

SUNDAY AFTERNOON.

When a man like Mr. Buchanan takes the measuring line of his powerful pen and indites a condemnation of Christianity, it were well to listen to what he has to say ! For however wrong he may be, what he says is for the most part beautifully said, and his opinion is shared by many who do not, who will not, or who cannot express it, but who share it none the less.

BAZAAR.

Mr. Buchanan's masterly production.   . The book should be read by everybody who admires and loves true poetry. We cannot attempt to review the ' Wandering Jew ' in these columns, and, so far, not a single criticism worth reading has appeared in the London press. Each man must read the book for himself.

MR. G. W. FOOTE.
(President of the National Secular Society.)

Mr. Buchanan's indictment of Christianity stands unanswered.

AGNOSTIC JOURNAL.

Mr. Buchanan's indictment is based upon the incontrovertible facts of history, and can neither be quashed nor repudiated.

REV. R. F. HORTON.

I rejoice in such attacks—stern, eloquent, and even bitter attacks are just what we should welcome. I do not understand the bitterness which some defenders of the faith have displayed towards Mr. Buchanan.

www.ingramcontent.com/pod-product-compliance
Lightning Source LLC
Chambersburg PA
CBHW030840270326
41928CB00007B/1149